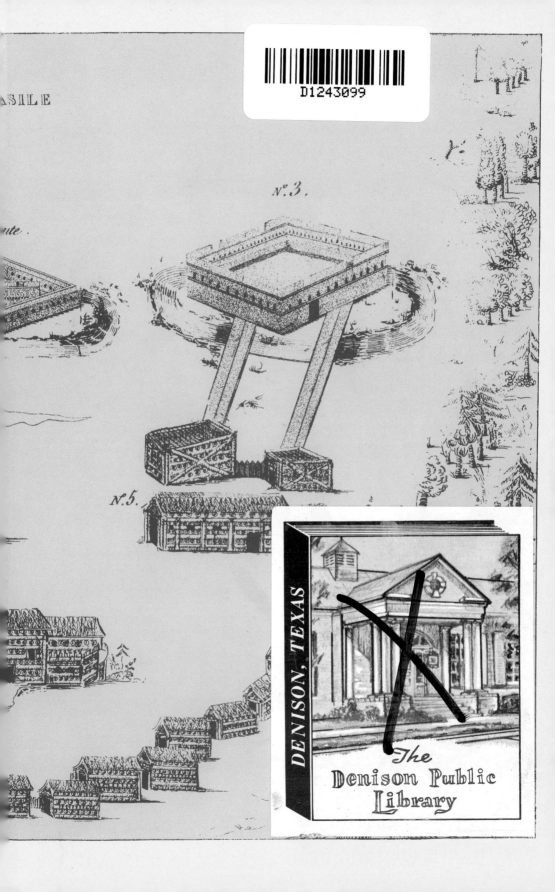

ASILE

N⁰.3.

N⁰.5.

The Story of Champ d' Asile

A FACSIMILE REPRODUCTION

The Story of Champ d'Asile

INTRODUCTION BY WILSON M. HUDSON

Steck-Vaughn Company

PUBLISHERS • AUSTIN, TEXAS

Steck-Vaughn's
Life and Adventure Series
Facsimiles and Reprints

Standard Book Number 8114-7696-0
Library of Congress Catalog Card Number 70-101370
PRINTED AND BOUND IN THE UNITED STATES OF AMERICA

A Facsimile Reproduction of the First Edition
New Material Copyright, 1969
STECK-VAUGHN COMPANY, PUBLISHERS
AUSTIN, TEXAS

Introduction

BY

WILSON M. HUDSON

The Book Club of Texas

The Story of Champ d'Asile was the seventh, final, and possibly most beautiful selection published by The Book Club of Texas. Despite the fact that publications of the Club were limited to only three hundred copies, the books won widespread acclaim for their design and production. Of the seven selections, three (the 1931, 1932, and 1933 choices) were named among the Fifty Books of the Year—a coveted honor awarded for quality of design, printing, paper, and binding. No other book club can boast such a record of designing and producing beautiful books.

The first selection, in 1930, was *Memoir of Colonel Ellis P. Bean,* designed and printed in Texas by the Rein Press of Houston. This volume was edited by H. K. Yoakum, whose name appears, by some curious error, as W. P. Yoakum on the title page.

The Club's second selection, *Eneas Africanus* by Harry Stillwell Edwards, appeared later in 1930. Though published in New York by the Marchbanks Press, it carried the following explanation: "As Mr. Marchbanks is a printer from Texas, The Book Club feels that the book may properly be called a native product."

Code Duello (1931), the third selection, designed and printed by the Lakeside Press of Chicago, was chosen as one of the Fifty Books of the Year. Compiled by Virginia Aylett Quitman McNealus, it was a series of previously unpublished letters—relating to a challenge to a duel—that had passed between Senator Sargeant S. Prentiss and Governor T. M. Tucker, both of Mississippi.

Like the third, the fourth publication, *Miss Zylphia Gant* by William Faulkner (1932), was honored as one of the Fifty Books of the Year. This very fine volume, consisting of a single short story, was designed, printed, and bound in Texas by a Dallas printer, J. M. Colville & Son.

v

The Club's fifth selection, *From Texas to Mexico and the Court of Maximilian in 1865* by Judge Alexander Watkins Terrell, was chosen as one of the Fifty Books of the Year for 1934. Designed and printed by the Lakeside Press of Chicago, it provided as an extra attraction a previously unpublished drawing by O. Henry.

The sixth selection was not offered until 1936, the centennial anniversary of Texas's independence. J. Frank Dobie's *Tales of the Mustang* was illustrated by Jerry Bywater and printed by the Rein Company of Houston.

The seventh and last selection of The Book Club of Texas, *The Story of Champ d'Asile,* was printed in 1937 by the Rydal Press of Santa Fe, New Mexico. It is reproduced here in facsimile as part of Steck-Vaughn's Life and Adventure Series.

In 1941 Stanley Marcus, founder and president of The Book Club of Texas, conveyed the funds in the Club's treasury and its unsold books to the Texas Folklore Society. The Society's minutes for that year state that it was not possible to sell the books at the inventoried price, but that the Society hoped to realize enough to publish a book worthy of the Club's achievement. With this help the Society was enabled to begin the Range Life Series. If the Society had any of the Club's books today, it could readily dispose of them for prices many times greater than those originally listed. A collector fortunate enough to locate a copy of *The Story of Champ d'Asile* would have to pay about $100 for it; he could not expect to obtain Faulkner's *Miss Zylphia Gant* for much less than $300, and he would have to go higher for Dobie's *Tales of the Mustang,* now the rarest of the Club's publications.

Mr. Marcus, prime mover in the establishment of the Club, had the assistance of John A. Lomax in the early stages. In August of 1928 Lomax, then associated with the Republic National Bank of Dallas, wrote to E. W. Winkler, librarian at The University of Texas, for a list of the principal librarians of Texas so that he could invite them to join the prospective organization. Though Lomax signed himself "Treasurer, The Book Club of Texas," the Club was not formally organized until the next year. As Mr. Marcus states ("The Book Club of Texas," *News Notes: Bulletin of the Texas Library Association,* X [Oct. 1934], 16), the question of a book club of Texas was asked "a small group of bibliophiles" in 1929,

vi

and The Book Club of Texas came into being. It was planned to publish at least one book a year on a literary or historical subject and to encourage the graphic arts generally in Texas. The material chosen was to be indigenous and preferably unpublished, and editions were to be limited to 300 copies. A very handsome broadside, printed by the Rein Company of Houston, announced the formation of the Club, stated its purposes and mode of operation, and listed the charter members. Dallas was better represented than any other Texas city, but there were also members from Austin, Houston, Galveston, and San Antonio. H. Y. Benedict, president of The University of Texas, and R. L. Batts, chairman of the board of regents, had enrolled, and so had W. J. Battle of the classics department and Fannie Ratchford of the Wrenn Library. J. Frank Dobie was not a charter member, but he joined shortly after the appearance of the Club's first book.

In republishing a facsimile edition of *The Story of Champ d'Asile*, Steck-Vaughn Company is rendering a service to students of history and literature and to book lovers. The only materials added to the original are facsimiles of the title page of each of the two original French books on which *The Story of Champ d'Asile* is based, and a facsimile of the map from Louis François L'Héritier's *Le Champ-d'Asile* published by Ladvocat in Paris in 1819. The title page of the original edition of *L'Héroïne* is reproduced on page 28. The title page of the original French edition of *Le Texas* is reproduced on page 106. The map is reproduced on page 26.

Rather than correct the occasional typographical errors, none of which produces a confusion of sense, the editors thought it best to reproduce the book in its original form. On page 126, for example, the period instead of a comma after "Perrey Point" would cause no difficulty for the reader.

The Book

The Story of Champ d'Asile brings together under a new title
two books published separately in Paris, both in 1819: *Le Texas,
ou notice historique sur le champ d'Asile* . . . by Hartmann and
Millard and *L'Héroïne du Texas* . . . by G . . .n F . . .n. *L'Héroïne*
is a fictionalized derivative of *Le Texas* with assistance from other
accounts of the French exiles in Texas. The title of *Le Texas* is in-
correctly given in Miss Ratchford's Preface.

Donald Joseph, who was teaching French at The University of
Texas, made the translation and Miss Ratchford revised it editori-
ally. Though acknowledging that she had introduced many changes,
she says that the translation is basically his. She states that
L'Héroïne had been "freely amended," but in fact it follows the
original rather closely except for the omission of several overly
rhetorical passages.

It must have been Miss Ratchford's preference of the literary to
the historical that led her to place *The Heroine* before *Texas* in the
book. She says *The Heroine* has a strong claim to be considered
the first Texas novel, but the characters do not even reach Texas
until three-fifths of the book has been narrated. Well over half is
given to the courtship of Edmund and Ernestine in France, related
in the delicate, genteel manner then in vogue. The author dis-
claims that his book is a novel; he says his facts are true, though he
has changed the names of his hero and heroine. These "facts," as
it appears in his Preface, have come from accounts of the exiles
published in Paris, which he asserts a right to use. Besides letters
by returned exiles in the newspapers, he mentions a work on Texas
brought out by the publisher Ladvocat in 1819 and the book by
Hartmann and Millard. Ladvocat's title was *Le Champ-d'Asile,
tableau topographique et historique du Texas* and the author has
been identified from his initials as Louis François L'Héretier.
Ladvocat was in the field before Hartmann and Millard (see their

allusion on page 112), and his book went to a second edition in the year of publication. Hartmann and Millard promised to tell the love story of Edouard and Adrienne, said to be two of the exiles, but they decided not to because such a romantic tale might have caused doubts about the strict truth of their narration and detracted from their avowed purpose of making clear why the colony failed (see their Epilogue). The anonymous author of *L'Héroïne du Texas* picked up and exploited their lead; he was able to recognize literary opportunity when it beckoned. It was easy for him to construct a novel about young lovers and attach it to the adventures of Napoleonic exiles in a strange land. He was evidently not one of the colonists; if he had been, he would surely have said so in his Preface.

Comparison of the French and English texts indicates that not every departure from *L'Héroïne* can be considered an emendation. When Edmund keeps looking for Ernestine everywhere and at the same time tries to conceal his feelings from her brother, the French reads thus: "Je la cherchais sans cesse. J'aurais voulu commander à mes désires, à mes regards, à mon impatience" (p. 28). The English combines the sentences and implies an erroneous connection: "I sought her out ceaselessly, wishing to secure command of my desire, my glance, and my impatience" (pp. 44-45). The contrast and the conditional idea have been lost; it would have been better to keep the second sentence separate and render it something like this: "I tried vainly to master my emotions, glances, and impatience."

When Edmund is talking to Ernestine's brother about asking her parents for her hand, the brother assures him that they will hear his proposal. Then Edmund asks (p. 65), without the initial quotation marks, "Do you think they will listen to me with favor?" This is a rendition of "Croyez-vous qu'elle me sera favorable?"— "Do you think she will be favorable to me?" Edmund was wondering what Ernestine's attitude would be. Mr. Joseph might have misread "elles" for "elle," but he could hardly have mistaken the singular for the plural verb. The change must have been editorial. Immediately afterward an impersonal *on* is translated as *they*, so that the pronoun seems to refer specifically to the opinion of Edmund held by Ernestine's parents instead of to that generally held ("l'estime qu'on a pour vous," p. 56).

"I am flying in the face of events that, in an hour perhaps, will decide my fate . . ." (p. 67) is not a possible translation of "Je cours au-devant des événemens [*sic*], et dans une heure peut-être ma destinée va être fixée. . ." (p. 59). Edmund means simply that he is getting ahead of events, wondering what will be the response to his proposal.

The reader will see at once that the word *later* in "her father, the later reigning supreme as General" (p. 77) should be *latter,* but he cannot tell that the passage is a garbling of ". . . il régnait, en général, une grande union parmi tous les colons" (p. 73). This should have been ". . . there existed, in general, a complete unity among the colonists."

Now and then the choice of words is unidiomatic or unhappy, as in "his remarks of me to them" (p. 34) or "a supernatural being you looked to my eyes" (p. 37). *About* should have been used instead of *of* and *appeared* instead of *looked.* On page 94 substitute *privation* for *poverty;* on page 96, *shelter* for *cabin;* on page 100, "in order not to endanger her life" for "if her health was not to be compromised."

Punctuation is not impeccable. American practice demands a comma after *charms* and a semicolon after *believe* in "equal to her charms of which she is neither vain nor proud" (p. 40) and "I spoke of it not badly, I believe, I saw my three traveling companions smile" (p. 44). No quotation marks should have been placed around the central paragraph on page 82; these are not the spoken words of anyone, but simply the narrator's apostrophe to the savior Indian. At the bottom of page 91 add quotation marks at the end of the paragraph purporting to be taken from the official's report.

In *The Heroine*'s version of how the Indian saved the exiles who had eaten what they thought to be an edible plant, it is said that he pressed the juice of the antidote into "un coco pendu à sa ceinture" (p. 82). To conceal the author's mistake of implying that coconuts grew along the Trinity, Mr. Joseph or Miss Ratchford substituted the general term *vessel* (p. 82) for *coco.* In her Introduction Miss Ratchford suggests that the poisonous plant was probably poke greens. It is not described in *L'Héroïne,* but Hartmann and Millard say it resembled lettuce. According to their account, the antidote was another plant, which had to be boiled. In *L'Héroïne* the antidote is "fruits en grappe" (p. 82), rendered as "bunches of fruit" (p. 82). Miss Ratchford's reconstruction in her Introduction has features from both *The Heroine* and *Texas*. At any rate, the Indian behaved exactly as a noble savage should; he produced the antidote at once and brought about a cure, for, as all herb doctors know, near every harmful plant there grows a beneficial plant with the power of counteracting its effects. The settlers of East Texas did not learn the antidote for poke greens from the Indians; instead, they parboiled the greens and poured off the liquid as the first step in preparing them. (See James W. Byrd, "Creeping Ignorance on Poke Sallet," *The Sunny Slopes of Long Ago* [Dallas, 1966], pp. 157-63.) The plain narrative of a rank-and-file member of the so-called colony, translated by Jack Autrey Dabbs (in "Additional Notes on Champ d'Asile," *Southwestern Historical Quarterly*, LIV [1950-51], 347-58), includes the poisoning incident but does not mention the timely arrival of the friendly Indian who knew just what to do.

The author of *L'Héroïne* speaks of hunting *cormorans* (p. 100) on Galveston Island for food. The translation has *cormorants* (p. 93); pelicans would have been the nearest thing to cormorants in this locality, but the exiles would hardly have been eating them when game and fish were plentiful. Here the translator does not shield the author as he does in the occurrence of *coco*. Since *L'Héroïne* was not based on firsthand knowledge, when the author went beyond his written sources, he was likely to make mistakes.

In *Le Texas* the situation is different. It is sometimes difficult to find the right English word for an animal or plant mentioned by Hartmann and Millard, but they seem to have some real knowledge of what they were writing about. When they say that the colonists caught mostly *coad-fish* (p. 62, italicized) in the Trinity River, they could not have meant *codfish*. They were using this as an English word. Had they confused it with *catfish*, which to a Frenchman would sound very much like *codfish*? They had probably fished in other American rivers where catfish were caught. Mr. Joseph wisely carries over the word as *coadfish* in italics (p. 139) without trying to translate it.

Hartmann and Millard say (p. 125) that three kinds of snakes are numerous in Texas. *Le serpen* [sic] *à sonnettes* is the ordinary

French designation for rattlesnake and presents no difficulties; *le congo* means the. congo eel, sometimes called the *congo snake,* and *le mangeur d'oeufs* would be some kind of egg-eating snake, popularly know as a *chicken snake.* Mr. Joseph translates the last two names literally—*the congo* and *the egg-eater* (p. 176).

Mr. Joseph carries over into his translation some names of Indian tribes (italicized) just as they appear in *Le Texas* without providing equivalents more familiar to his readers. It would have been helpful to substitute the forms ordinarily used by writers in English, which he could have discovered by consulting the list of variant names in Hodge's *Handbook of American Indians.* These are equivalents, Hartmann and Millard's form on the left and Hodge's on the right:

Alabamos	Alibamu
Camanches	Comanche
Chactas	Choctaw
Cochatis	Koasati
Dankhaves	Tonkawa
Karankavès	Karankawa
Panis	Pawnee
Tankards	Tonkawa

Hodge does not add *s* to show the plural, though it is now general usage to do so. For many readers *Coushatta* would be more recognizable than *Koasati* because of the well-known Alabama-Coushatta reservation in East Texas. The Indian with the timely antidote was said to be a Coushatta.

Joseph and Ratchford's practice for the French *Naquidoches* is variable. In *Texas* the word occurs as *Naquidoche* (p. 132), *Nacogdoches* (p. 163), and *Naquidoches* (p. 177), all unitalicized. Hodge spells the name of the Indians without an *s,* but the town, named for the Indians, is *Nacogdoches.* Readers will be puzzled by the statement that the colonists had "made several plantings of Naquidoche, which did very well . . ." (p. 132). A phrase in the original—"de tabac" (p. 43)—was omitted in translation; what was planted was tobacco of the kind raised by the Nacogdoches Indians.

Place-names are very troublesome to a translator when his original deals with newly explored country and antedates the existence of a reliable map. All he can do is to correlate the names as he finds them with the later, accepted names and point out the difficulties whenever correlation is not possible. It is difficult to deal with geographical perplexities without some form of notes, and Joseph and Ratchford have none. They carry over into their text, without comment, the mysterious *rivière Barosso* of *Le Texas*, spelled *Barosso* on page 176 and *Baosso* on page 177. This is the Brazos. The geography is not very clear, but there is no other large river which "flows into the Gulf of Mexico near Galveston Bay" and which has a name sounding like the Spanish *Brazos*. L'Héretier uses the form *Brassas* in *Le Champ-d'Asile* (p. 64). The map which Ladvocat had made for the book shows a *Barroso* flowing into Galveston Bay east of the Trinity and joined to it above as if it were another mouth. (Ladvocat's map is reproduced on page 26.)

Ladvocat's map, said to be based on materials obtained from "one of the principal colonists," reflects the hazy conception which the French had of the region in 1819. Besides being incomplete and sketchy, it contains copyist's errors such as *Baralaria* for *Barataria* and *Careusin* for something like *Carasiu* (*Carcassiou* in *Le Texas*, p. 103). Nevertheless, with this inexact map it is possible to follow the overland journey of the colonists from Galveston to New Orleans. For the benefit of their readers Joseph and Ratchford should have used *Calcasieu* instead of *Carcassiou* and *Mermentau* instead of *Mermentas* (p. 164). They could have supplied modern equivalents for most of the other unfamiliar place-names. The *Toya* mentioned in *Texas* (p. 177) is the *Attoyac*, despite the geographical inaccuracy of the sentence in which it occurs.

It would hardly be good practice to respell personal names that have been taken over into French, though the reader of *Texas* may be startled to see the name *Waskès* attributed to a Spanish colonel (p. 136). The colonel's wife is referred to later as *Madame Vasquez* (p. 170).

Le Texas was subjected to some editorial emendation, though not to so much as *L'Héroïne*. The apostrophe to women on page 78 of *Le Texas* was evidently thought to be too mawkish for inclusion, and so it was dropped without indication (p. 150). Nor is it indicated that details about General Rigaud's daughter and son were revised (p. 179) according to handwritten changes appearing in the copy of *Le Texas* (p. 130) which Joseph was using.

Texas contains fewer inexact or erroneous renderings than does *The Heroine*. At the top of page 108 there is a passage confused in sense and grammar: ". . . the refuge which you had been pleased to imagine would see the peaceful end of our days which has been but too long and stormy." The French (third page, unnumbered, of dedicatory epistle) is perfectly clear and easily translatable: ". . . the refuge where you had hoped that our days, too long tempestuous, would run their course in peace." Sometimes the tense is altered and sometimes a cognate in French produces a peculiar expression in English: ". . . et nous étions forcés de convenir que le sexe le plus faible trouvait des forces qui quelquefois nous abandonnaient" (p. 78) becomes ". . . and we are forced to admit that the so-called weaker sex possessed a strength which at times abandoned us " (p. 150). Change *are* to *were* and *abandoned* to *deserted*—and cancel the intrusive *so-called*. Mr. Joseph preferred to retain the French *eau-de-vie* instead of using the simple English word *brandy*, with the result that two typographical errors slipped by the editor, *eaude vin* (p. 150) and *eau de vin* (p. 153). Errors of this kind puzzle the reader for a moment, but he can soon supply the correction. He has no means of correcting the kind of error which occurs on page 168 when two sentences beginning with dates become confused. The Scilly Islands were sighted on the 6th of May, not the 3rd; what happened on the 3rd has dropped out—a meeting with an English corvette (pp. 109-10). This is the only error of fact in *Texas* for which the translator or editor is responsible, and it is not very significant. More could be said about accuracy and expression in Joseph and Ratchford's *Texas*, but there is no reason for doing so.

Translators are always open to criticism, particularly in matters of exactness and idiom. The shortcomings of *The Story of Champ d'Asile* do not seriously impair the value or interest of the book for the general reader.

WILSON M. HUDSON
Austin, Texas
July 20, 1969

xiv

The Story of
CHAMP D'ASILE

First View of Aigleville
Colony of Texas or Champ d'Asile

THE STORY OF
CHAMP D'ASILE

AS TOLD BY TWO OF THE COLONISTS

Translated from the French by
Donald Joseph and Edited
with an Introduction by
Fannie E. Ratchford

THE BOOK CLUB OF TEXAS
1620-26 MAIN STREET : DALLAS TEXAS

A FACSIMILE REPRODUCTION

STECK-VAUGHN COMPANY, AUSTIN, TEXAS

A Facsimile Reproduction of the First Edition
New Material Copyright, 1969
STECK-VAUGHN COMPANY, PUBLISHERS
AUSTIN, TEXAS

Affectionately inscribed to
Mattie Austin Hatcher, one time
Archivist of the University of Texas,
who first directed my attention
to this story

Preface

The story of Champ d'Asile was brought to my knowledge a number of years ago by Mrs. Mattie Austin Hatcher, Archivist in The University of Texas. In response to my interest, Donald Joseph of the French Department of The University of Texas translated from the French three accounts of the ill-fated colony, hoping to publish them as a triology consisting of an historical narrative, a love story, and a semifictitious adventure. The plan came to naught chiefly because of literary faults in the originals, which Mr. Joseph did not feel at liberty to correct.

From this group, *L'Heroine du Texas* is now selected and freely emended, as the most interesting for publication, adding, as it does, the charm of a Rousseauan love story to an historical document. It has, moreover, a strong claim to the title, *The First Texas Novel*.

The editor has made no attempt to relate Champ d'Asile to earlier French activities in Texas. That work is being done by an able scholar. The present volume is offered merely as a good story of a highly romantic and little known episode in Texas history: the futile attempt of a group of French exiles to found a Napoleonic state in the Southwestern wilderness.

Neither the author of the novel nor its hero and heroine have been identified from the available list of Champ d'Asile colonists. Hartmann and Millard, in *Le Texas du Notice Historique sur Champ d'Asile*, call the lovers Edward and Adrianne. So much does the Hartmann and Millard narrative add to the present story that an abbreviated version of it is given as a supplement or glorified footnote.

No material remains have been discovered to fix the site of Champ d'Asile. Tradition places it in the near vicinity of the present town of Liberty, a name inherited, it is claimed, directly from the French fort.

For help in preparing this brief and simple work thanks are due to Donald Joseph, the real "founder of the feast," for the translation, despite many changes, is basically his; to W.E.Wrather for generous loans of his books on Champ d'Asile and the aquatints here reproduced; and to Joseph O. Naylor for his courteous release of the Introduction which was originally written for *The Epic Century*.

Frances Ratchford
The University of Texas

Introduction

More than a century ago, and two years before Stephen F. Austin brought his first Anglo-Americans to the Brazos and Colorado Rivers, a Frenchman on the Seine wrote, apropos of a flood of publications hot from the press, "Texas has become a rich field for literature and anyone may exploit it." He might have cited among a host of lesser tillers of the soil the poet Béranger and, a few years later, the novelist Balzac.

The occasion for the outburst was the founding of a colony of Napoleonic exiles on the bank of the Trinity River in the heart of the Texas wilderness. Such a demonstration of the Rousseauan doctrine of return to nature was enough in itself to excite the interest of romantic France: joined to patriotism and national pride it aroused an enthusiasm that swept the nation, expressing itself in public subscription, benefit performances at the theaters, literary productions, and pictorial delineations of imaginary scenes in the far-off colony. The settlement was a New World Utopia which roused exhausted France from the lethargy of Bourbon reaction to a momentary flash of youthful hope.

Strangely enough, the episode that so excited the mother country and gave the diplomats of three nations some bad moments, making itself felt even in lonely St. Helena, has failed to find a place in the traditions of the land where it

9

was enacted. Texas people and Texas literature have forgotten that Texas forests, lighted by the campfires of Napoleon's Old Guard, once rang to shouts of "Vive L'Empereur." Anglo-Texans have never sung, "The laurel grows in Champ d'Asile." But for contemporary narratives the incident would be entirely lost. Those who would know the story must seek it, still in the mother tongue of the writers, on closely guarded shelves of collectors and in "rare book rooms" of public libraries.

What to do with the imperial officers was a problem confronting the restored Bourbon government at the end of the Hundred Days. Napoleon had chosen the United States of America as a place of retirement for himself and his family, and might easily have reached that land of refuge but for his indecision of action and his reluctance to accept the appearance of flight. Joseph Bonaparte, ex-King of Spain, was the only member of the family to enter the designated haven, he alone obtaining the passport necessary for leaving France.

The two, Napoleon and Joseph, were together at Rochefort for a number of days before the Emperor "threw himself upon the generosity of the British nation," by surrendering to Captain Maitland of the *Bellerophon*. In the course of that time Joseph exhausted in vain every persuasion to bring his brother to accept his passport and quarters in the brig *Commerce* which was to take him to America—the resemblance between the two being close enough to insure success of the exchange. It was not until after the *Bellerophon* had sailed that Joseph completed arrangements for his own departure for the United States.

The American brig, *Charleston*, of South Carolina, was chartered for himself and a small party formerly connected with Napoleon's court. They sailed on July 25, 1815, and landed safely at New York on August 28. In America Joseph called himself Count de Surveilliers, though his identity was well known. After creating a small flurry in diplomatic circles by a not very persistent effort to obtain an interview with President Madison, he settled down for a few months in New York before he leased "Landsowne," the Bingham estate on the Schuylkill. Finding this too near Philadelphia and lacking the seclusion he sought, he purchased a farm of about two hundred acres, called "Point Breeze," near Bordentown, New Jersey. On this estate, enlarged by successive purchases, he remained until his return to Europe in 1832, "living quietly and unostentatiously the life of a private citizen. . . ." His home was the center of generous hospitality for all French exiles, and many are the stories of his kindness to even the humblest of his fellow countrymen. Around him the faithful rallied, and to him they paid the court once accorded his brother.

The fortunes of Napoleon's followers in France fell into the shifty hands of that master of intrigue, Joseph Fouché, Duke of Otranto. On the second abdication of Napoleon he was elected President of the Provisional Commission, and was retained by Louis XVIII, as Minister of Police, for this disagreeable task. He it was who made up the first proscription list of about one hundred names, many of them his former colleagues, accomplices, and agents. Under the scrutiny of the King and his council the list was reduced to fifty-nine. As each name was confirmed, Fouché, with his usual double-dealing, perhaps this time with the sanction of the King, warned the victim and provided passports and money for escape. Only those who failed to accept the proffered warning were arrested. Among the refugees to America were five who became the leading spirits of the exiles, though their number included hundreds of lower rank, who for one reason and another had found it desirable to leave France: the brothers Lallemand, Charles the elder, who had begged and been refused permission to share Napoleon's exile, and Henri; Marshal Grouchy, with his two sons, Colonels Alphonse and Victor; General Lefebvre-Desnouëttes; and General Rigaud.

Their reception in the United States was in the main kind and sympathetic. Earlier dislike of Napoleon was counterbalanced by the reactionary policy of the restored Bourbons, and the wave of good feeling that swept the country toward the end of Madison's administration tended to replace political animosities with benevolent understanding. There were already in the country, particularly in Philadelphia and Baltimore, a goodly number of French refugees from the Negro insurrection in Santo Domingo of almost a quarter century earlier. These were, for the most part, in moderate circumstances, and they gave their countrymen a warm welcome which included hospitality and financial assistance to such as needed it. Some of the refugees brought considerable means with them, which they shared with the less fortunate. In the course of time, however, dependence became a burden to both donors and recipients. It was to the interest of all that the refugees become self sustaining. The Government was besought to give them homes in a climate similar to that of France, where they might cultivate the most familiar products of their country—the vine and the olive.

A company of the exiles was organized at Philadelphia in

December, 1816, and members of their group were sent out to find a suitable situation for a colony. Acting on advice rather than first-hand investigation, they petitioned Congress to grant them a tract on the Tombigbee River, in the Mississippi Territory recently acquired by treaty from the Creek Indians. The request was granted on liberal terms: they were given four contiguous townships, each six miles square, at $2.00 per acre, to be paid over a period of fourteen years. The land was to be divided among two hundred and eighty settlers, no one to hold more than six hundred and forty acres. The society was to select its own agent.

General Charles Lallemand was chosen president of the group, which was variously styled "Society for the Cultivation of the Vine and Olive," "The French Emigrant Society," and "The Tombigbee Association." The first group of settlers, about one hundred and fifty in number, left Philadelphia in December, 1817, and others followed late in April of the next year, taking with them vines and olive trees for planting.

The colony was a failure for the obvious reason that its members were soldiers unable to adapt themselves to civil pursuits. None among them knew anything of agriculture even in their own country, and all were entirely ignorant of conditions in their new homes. The bill of grant had been formulated with paritcular care to prevent speculation in the designated lands, but it utterly failed of its purpose. Money lenders owned most of the ground before the first of the exiles reached it. The only achievement of the colonists as a group was the laying out of a town called Aigleville, which proved to be outside their boundaries. And a fairly large and pretentious house built by the leader,

13

General Lefebvre-Desnouëttes, on his tract of five hundred acres was the only considerable improvement made by an individual. Near by the General built a log "sanctuary," the shrine of a large bronze statue of Napoleon; "around its feet were swords and pistols which Desnouëttes had taken in battle, together with beautiful flags, tastefully hung around the walls." Desnouëttes' wife was a sister of the famous Parisian banker, La Fitte. From her he received large sums of money for France. It is said that he spent twenty-five thousand dollars in opening and cultivating his farm in Alabama.

By the end of the summer of 1818, the company was broken up, and most of its members back in Philadelphia. General Charles Lallemand, the president of the company, in all probability, never visited the Tombigbee, for while that settlement was in formation, he was in New Orleans purchasing supplies for his own colony in Texas. His ambitions transcended a mere agricultural colony within the United States. That it included the rehabilitation of the Bonaparte fortunes in Latin America and the rescue of Napoleon from St. Helena was believed by many of his contemporaries. It is certain that those of the Old Guard in America never ceased to hope for Napoleon's escape, and talked of it and planned for it each time they came together. No scheme was too absurd for their consideration. Just as the royal family of Portugal, driven from its throne by the usurpations of Napoleon, fled overseas to the colony of Brazil, so might Joseph Bonaparte, deposed king of Spain, set up his standard in the Spanish colonies of America until the way was open for his return to his European court. Once established on the throne of Mexico, he would rescue his brother.

The scheme was set forth in a letter from London in July,

1816, published in Nile's Register, but denounced as false by the editor of the magazine. In the late summer of 1817, Hyde de Neuville, representative of the restored Bourbon government in Washington, came into possession of a disturbing set of papers apparently written by Lakenal, a proscribed regicide whom Lafayette had introduced to Jefferson as a "Member of the French Institute, Officer of the University, and Inspector-General of the new Metrical System, who abandons those functions and a handsome treatment to become a settler in the State of Kentucky." These papers implied the existence in America of an association under the name of the "Napoleonic Confederacy," conspiring to place Joseph Bonaparte in control of Mexico as King of Spain and the Indies.

The documents, with a note from De Neuville, were laid before President Madison, who instituted the desired investigation. De Neuville also informed Spanish Minister Onis of the plot against the Mexican possessions of the King of Spain, and Onis in his turn laid his complaint before the Secretary of State, hoping that the United States would not violate its treaty of neutrality with European powers by allowing the execution of such a plot within its borders.

An investigation failed to show that Joseph Bonaparte, or the *Count de Surveillers*, as he was called, had contributed either money or encouragement to the scheme. Lallemand, whose name had been connected with the affair, went to Washington and there obtained an interview with Secretary Adams, in which he denied acquaintance with Lakenal, as well as any knowledge of the alleged plot, the report of which, he surmised, had grown out of the project settlement on the Tombigbee River. The report, however, reached St.

Helena by way of England and led to a stricter watch over the imperial prisoner.

On December 17, 1817, a few days after the departure of the Tombigbee colonists from Philadelphia, a second group of exiles under the leadership of General Rigaud, set sail on the schooner *Huntress* carrying a cargo that accorded strangely with the needs of an agricultural colony. Included were six hundred muskets, four hundred sabres, and twelve thousand pounds of powder. Nicolas Biddle of Philadelphia reported to President Monroe that the vessel carried one hundred and fifty men, chiefly Frenchmen, who had been disciplined and prepared by the Lallemands. It was said, Biddle wrote, that other vessels from other ports would join them at some point, most probably in the Gulf of Mexico. It was said also that the funds for the expedition were raised almost entirely from land given to the officers and men in Alabama, which they sold at $1.00 or $1.50 per acre, chiefly to French people of Philadelphia. In one of the narratives of the expedition it is stated that these supplies were bought "partly with the voluntary contribution of the colonists and partly with a donation of Joseph Bonaparte."

A suspicion occurred to President Monroe, which he expressed to Biddle, that the expedition might in reality have been prompted by Spanish Minister Onis against the United States. Biddle was sure that this was not true, though he thought that the brothers Lallemand might be open to offers from Onis for their services with the Royalists.

The division of the expedition carried by the *Huntress* was under the command of General Rigaud, who was accompanied by his daughter. The ship sailed south from Philadelphia, rounded the Tortugas, and in the vicinity of

New Orleans was visited by an officer of one of Jean Lafitte's independent corsairs from Galveston Island. The meeting was altogether friendly, and the courtesies exchanged on board were continued on shore at Galveston, where the colonists remained for more than a month, waiting for the arrival of General Lallemand with supplies and recruits.

One of the narrators depicts Lafitte's band as a bad lot: "freebooters gathered from among all the nations of the earth and determined to put into practice the traditions of the buccaneers of old. They gave themselves up to the most shameless debauchery and disgusting immorality, and only their chief by his extraordinary strength and indomitable resolution had the slightest control over their wild and savage natures. Thanks to him the pirates became harmless neighbors to the exiles, with whom they often exchanged words of political sympathy, crying amicably, 'Long live Liberty!'"

Lallemand's arrival with additional colonists in early March was hailed with delight; songs of glory were sung, and toasts were drunk to the fatherland and the friends who remained there, and to the good fortune and prosperity of the colony. The recruits showed a motley mingling of French exiles—Tombigbee colonists and Santo Dominican refugees—Spaniards, Poles, Mexicans, and Americans, with a sprinkling of ex-pirates. The company, now numbering about four hundred members, set out in high spirits for the chosen site on the Trinity River. Boats had been purchased from Lafitte—one narrator says ten, another twenty-four. A storm scattering the craft, most of them had to turn back to Galveston. One was wrecked, drowning five of the six men on board.

17

After three days of struggle on the water, the party came together at Point Perrey, there they decided to separate: one group of a hundred, led by Generals Lallemand and Rigaud, to continue the journey by land; the rest, under Colonel Charrasin, to bring up the supplies by boat, guided by Indians with whom the colonists had already established friendly relations, "thanks to a few bottles of rum and some knives and muskets." The boats missed the mouth of the river and were six days in reaching the designated site "twenty leagues from the Gulf of Mexico." In the meanwhile the overland party, having taken insufficient food with them, suffered cruelly. In their hunger they ate of a wild plant resembling lettuce (probably poke greens) which they found in the wood—all except Lallemand, Rigaud, and Dr. Mann, the surgeon. An hour after this ill-advised repast, every one who had tasted it, ninety-seven in number, "lay stretched on the ground in awful agony, wracked by the most terrible convulsions." As they lay "pale and undone," an Indian of the "Cochatis nation" appeared. The sight of the sufferers and uneaten portions of the herb told him the story. He disappeared into the forest and shortly returned with bunches of fruit. Pressing the juice from these into a vessel carried at his waist, he gave it to the sufferers to drink. "They soon began to stir and rise as if from a long painful fainting spell."

On the sixth day the land party met the flotilla bearing provisions at the appointed place. They had been four days without food and were in an exhausted condition, but recovered rapidly.

The first concern of the united colonists was the erection of fortifications, followed as soon as possible by the building of private homes for the married men and higher officers.

The settlement was laid out on a circular plan, taking its direction from the four forts. The dwellings were built of trees of medium thickness, cut into lengths of from six to seven feet, driven into the ground close together, and the chinks filled with a mud plaster. Loop-holes were left in the walls, so that each dwelling might be used as a fortress in case of attack.

Their completion was marked by gay house warmings, when the men who built them fêted the mistresses, drinking to Texas, to the Sons of Glory, and to the happiness of the French people.

The settlement was called Champ d'Asile.

From this place General Lallemand issued a manifesto, dated May 11, 1818, in which he announced to the world the establishment of an argicultural colony, claiming "the first right given by God to man—that of settling in this country, clearing it, and using the produce which nature never refuses to the patient laborer"; and disclaiming any warlike intentions, except defense against attack.

The code of laws as drawn up "was founded on justice, friendship, and disinterestedness," the fundamental principle being the obligation of mutual aid and protection. All property was held in common, and all looked "to the same end in making the colony prosper: the general happiness, which would rebound to the individual happiness of each."

Lallemand's proclamation made a great noise in Europe, above all, in France, exciting the admiration of the Liberals and the sneers of the opposing party. *La Minerve*, a fortnightly review of the day opened a subscription list for the exiles which yielded approximately one hundred thousand francs.

Béranger contributed a highly romantic poem to the cause; a pamphlet written by Monsieur Shiritiar and published by Ladrocat, went through two editions; theatrical performances and various other benefits also brought in considerable money, not a cent of which reached the colonists.

The romantic nature of the exiles responded warmly to the natural beauty of their surroundings. The women transplanted flowers and cultivated them with care in gardens near their homes. They were particularly fond of the laurel, a "tree so beloved of the French that one might believe that it was for them alone that nature decorated the earth with it." Its abundance in the Texas woods was taken as a good omen by the exiles, and one of their number, the wife of an officer, composed a song having for its refrain, "The Laurel Grows in Champ d'Asile."

Far from cultivating the soil, the exiles, most of them totally ignorant of agriculture and uninterested in civil pursuits, were finding what diversion they could in military maneuvers after their hours of communal labor. They ate at a common mess, and bivouacked as if they were in an enemy's country, all except the Generals, two or three superior officers, and the women, who had large and not uncomfortable cabins. The few who cultivated gardens were richly rewarded for their efforts.

Besides drilling, the men had hunting, fishing, and athletic games for amusement. To all these diversions the few women and children of the colony lent their presence, commending all efforts and applauding success. The echoes of Texas resounded with songs of love and glory, the favorite on every occasion being "The Laurel Grows in Champ d'Asile."

Around the nightly campfire, kept burning to frighten

away wild beasts, the men loved to pretend they were loungers in the arcades of the *Palais Royal*, enjoying the glories of Imperial victories. Lallemand sometimes joined them, and entertained them with scraps of his last conversations with the Emperor. At such times the wildest dreams took possession of their imaginations, and Texas vanished from their thoughts. "They were eager to serve under the Mexican flag and help that country to throw off the Spanish yoke, after which they could easily persuade the Mexicans to give them a fast sailer, with which they would storm the island of St. Helena, carry off the Emperor in triumph, and crown him ruler of Mexico."

When such amusements as the camp itself could provide began to pall, Lallemand arranged a grand celebration in honor of a treaty made with several tribes of neighboring Indians, at which a deal of rum was distributed, until in a burst of drunken friendliness the Indians adopted Lallemand as a great chief and invested him "with the appropriate insignia of his new honors."

But nothing could stay the catastrophe inherent in the situation. Just as the expedition was setting out General Lallemand had issued a proclamation, a copy of which he claimed to have sent Ferdinand VII of Spain, arrogantly announcing his intention to make a settlement in Texas whether it pleased the Spanish court or no.

No one should have been surprised when friendly Indians brought information that a Spanish army was on its way from San Antonio to expel the French as hostile intruders. Prudence prevailed, and the colonists decided to withdraw, rather than to fight. Their departure was saddened by the slaying of two of their number by Indians. The partially devoured, still quivering bodies, were recovered and given burial. Dropping a laurel branch in their graves was the final pageant of Champ d'Asile.

There were enough boats at hand to take the company as far as Galveston, where they again established themselves as neighbors to the pirates. There scurvy, dysentery, and fever broke out, aggravated by lack of medicine and scarcity of food, and again they were at the mercy of the outlaws who drove hard bargains for all they sold.

The United States since the purchase of Louisiana 1803 had maintained a more or less definitely asserted claim to Texas, growing out of the vagueness of the Louisiana boundary as defined in the several treaties between France and Spain before the United States acquired Louisiana. The Spanish Minister Onis could not, without admitting this claim, protest to the government of the United States against the landing of the Napoleonic refugees at Galveston, but he did complain to President Adams of the apparent violation of neutrality in allowing the *Huntress* to be armed and equipped, as he claimed, in an American port.

Adams, without answering Onis' note, sent George Graham, chief clerk and acting Secretary of War during the last two years of Madison's administration, to Galveston to find out what Lallemand's expedition amounted to. Graham met the refugees from Champ d'Asile on Galveston Island, and he must have smiled sadly to himself at the Spanish Minister's fear of this pathetic group. When he departed, after consultation with Lallemand, the General-in-Chief and his staff went with him as far as New Orleans for the purpose of securing relief for his colonists.

In Lallemand's absence Rigaud assumed command of the

disheartened and almost desperate company. The pinch of hunger grew more desperate every day. Many were saved from starvation only by the generosity of Lafitte. To add to the situation, an agent of the Spanish Government appeared with the demand that the miserable wanderers quit Galveston Island. They replied that they could not treat with him in the absence of Lallemand. Day after day the relief their chief promised them was delayed. Then came a furious storm and a flood, such as swept the island in 1900, submerging the camp and huts to a depth of five feet. The remaining stores of the refugees were destroyed, and their suffering became intense. Immediate departure was imperative. The "perfect union and harmony" which up to this time had existed in the group went to the winds and each began to think how he might save himself. "Some wanted to join the settlers on the island; others wanted to go to New Orleans, while still others thought of other American cities. France was the objective of most."

A few of the group did join Lafitte's band of pirates; many crossed to the mainland and proceeded on foot, some to Alexandria, Louisiana; others to Nacogdoches; but the majority walked the one hundred and fifty leagues to New Orleans, supporting themselves solely by hunting. Those who remained behind, including Rigaud and his daughter, were furnished with a ship by Lafitte, together with such supplies as he could spare—a prize captured from the Spanish, the *St. Anthony de Compeachy*—in which they finally reached New Orleans after a trying voyage.

From New Orleans most of the colonists returned to France; a few, it is said, joined the Spanish revolutionists.

General Charles Lallemand lived out the varied life of an

adventurer and soldier of fortune, often in great poverty, until the Revolution of 1830 offered the chance to return to France—by Napoleon's will he had been left one hundred thousand francs. In 1832 he took his seat in the French Council of Peers, and, as a just reward for his faithfulness to Napoleon, he became military commander of Corsica. He died at Paris in 1839. His younger brother, Henri had, just before the Texas expedition, married a niece and one of the heiresses of Stephen Girard, rich merchant of Philadelphia, which explains why he was not of the Texas company. Rigaud remained in New Orleans and died there in 1820, not knowing that he, too, shared in Napoleon's will to the extent of one hundred thousand francs.

Fannie E. Ratchford
Austin, Texas
October 7, 1936

NOTE: The publications concerning the Champ d'Asile colony vary among themselves in many particulars, and all show departures from authentic documents. The accounts of the colony consulted for this summary are: Girard, Just: "The Adventures of a French Captain," translated by Lady Blanche Murphy (largely fiction); Hartmann et Millard: "Le Texas ou Notice Historique sur Champ d'Asile;" "Le Champ d'Asile a Texas ou Notice Curius et Interesante, par C—D—"; "Le Champ d'Asile, Tableau Topographique et historique du Texas par L.F. L'H"; and "L'Heroine du Texas, ou voyage de Madame *** aux Etats-Unis et au Mexique par Mr. G. . .n F. . .n"; Reeves, Jesse S.: "The Napoleonic Exiles in America; and miscellaneous materials in the Bibliotheque Nationale and Archives du Ministere des Affaires Etrangères.

Contents

❦ ❦ ❦

Illustrations

Explanation of the Plate

1. Dwelling of General Charles Lallemand. 2. Fort Charles. 3. Fort Henry. 4. Fort Stockade. 5. Dwelling of General Rigaud. 6. Storehouse. 7. Dwelling of the Colonel. 8. Trinity River.

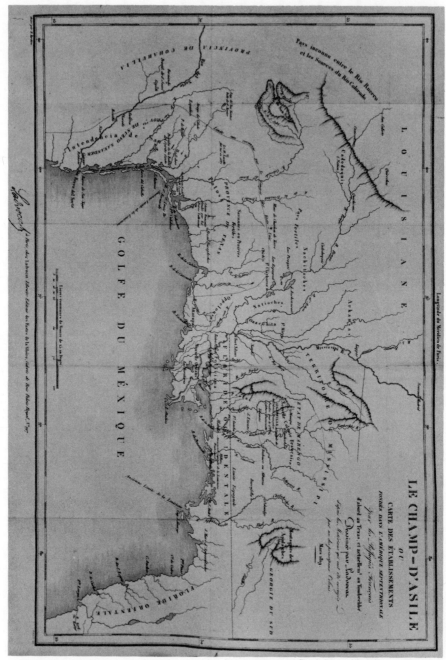

Facsimile of the Map from *Le Champ-d'Asile*.

The Heroine of Texas

by

G . . . . n F . . . . n

L'HÉROÏNE

DU TEXAS,

OU

VOYAGE DE MADAME ***

AUX ÉTATS-UNIS ET AU MEXIQUE.

Orné d'une Gravure représentant le Champ d'Asile
et le Camp retranché des Français.

Cet Ouvrage est terminé par une Romance.

PAR Mr G...n. F......n.

A PARIS,

Chez PLANCHER, Éditeur du Manuel des Braves,
rue Poupée, n° 7.
TxU

1819.

Facsimile of the Title Page of the Original French Edition of
L'Héroïne.

Editor's Preface

This work, whatever be the judgment which may be formed of it, is not a *novel*. The facts set down here are *true*, except that *Ernestine* and *Edmund* are not the names of my hero and heroine; I have thought it best to change them.

If there are persons who charge that I have made use of information already set down by others, I shall answer them as follows: Texas has become a rich field and anyone may exploit it. The newspapers have published various letters recounting events which transpired there: each colonist or refugee may on his return to France have his story of it printed, without anyone having the right to accuse him of plagiarism. The facts will be the same; the editing alone will offer variations. I have obtained details in this way, and I have used them; I have enlarged or modified them according to my taste, and I have turned them to account in the most advantageous way for the success of the work which I offer to the public.

M. Ladvocat brought out, sometime ago, a work on Texas. In it, he gave, on pages 25 and following, some information on the geographical situation of this province.

Messrs. Hartmann and Millard, members of the Champ d'Asile colony, but lately returned to France, have just published an historical treatise on that which they took part in or observed. I have looked through these two works: many of the details are the same; the style alone is different, and the resemblance between the two accounts is much more striking on page 1 2 2 *et seq.* where these gentlemen speak of the soil and the products—in a word, of everything which shows the resemblance between this country and Mexico.

M. Ladvocat, who had the advantage of priority, could then assail them. They could answer: we were on the ground; he could reply: I published my work before yours and etc., a series of interminable discussions. On all sides one would hear repeated with more or less vigor: *I have pillaged, thou hast pillaged, he has pillaged.* Well! Gentlemen! A fourth, more reasonable and cooler, would say to them, *We have all stolen:* let us sell, believe me, in peace, our more or less true stories about Texas. That is what should concern us. The essential point is to have a big sale and to secure the honor of a second edition.

As to the claims which historians of Texas—present or to be—could make, they will be answered as simply as naturally: *"Everyone at this business*
Can fruitlessly waste ink and paper."

I come back to the question in hand. It shall perhaps be urged against me that I have enlarged too much on the loves of Edmund and Ernestine; I answer that these developments seemed necessary to me, and that having omitted nothing of all that happened in Texas from the arrival of the French refugees in Champ d'Asile to their departure, I thought that the first duty of an historian was to portray in all their beauty and heroism the graces, glory and virtue of the exiles, and that this was the surest means of commending myself, as well as my work, to the indulgence of the readers.

The Heroine of Texas

THE EMIGRATION OF A GREAT number of Frenchmen to the United States and the gathering of a group of them on the banks of the Trinity River in the province of Texas, where they proposed to found a colony under the name of Champ d'Asile, aroused considerable interest in their favor. The French who remained in the mother country had seen with sorrow, but with admiration, that friends and brothers, after the storm, were determined to found a new fatherland on another hemisphere. Among the group were those brave men who for twenty-five years astonished the world by their brilliant exploits, now, and as if to obtain additional glory in the eyes of their contemporaries and posterity, thought to civilize a savage country and cultivate a virgin soil. Everyone wished the new colony success and prosperity.

It was with pleasure that the French at home learned that Champ d'Asile was to be founded; and it was with satisfaction, slightly mixed with pride, that they saw about to be demonstrated the saying that, *to Frenchmen,* "*Everything is possible.*" The vindication of this truth flattered the egotism of a nation known for its elevation of soul, its innate love of glory, and its penchant for great deeds. The interest grew when it was known that women had followed the fortunes of the refugees, undeterred by the weakness of their sex. Their strength of character and fortitude held them close to those with whom they had fearlessly cast their lot, hoping to enrich their lives and sweeten their memories and regrets, if perchance they should become homesick for their country. Love and attachments moved some; filial devotion, others; all had a motive worthy of praise and of respect.

So long as the life of the colony was calm and untroubled, while its early happiness was undisturbed, these faithful helpmates of our generous brothers exhibited only those sweet virtues which constitute the charm of domestic life. When hatred and persecutions—cruel daughters of passion— aroused the countries adjacent to Texas, and threatened the expulsion of the colonists from their new fatherland, the French women, so worthy of their high name, gave proof that their courage was equal to that of their husbands, relatives, and friends, and their strength grew in proportion to their need.

It is of one of these women that I am going to tell my readers, and in her I shall show heroism combined with beauty, virtue, and talents, and all the happy, rare, and precious qualities which go to make up the woman whom nature has chosen as a model closest approaching ideal perfection.

Ernestine, Edmund, you whose friend I was, you whose pleasures I have shared—but above all the pain and the dangers—you who gave me so often through example the strength to bear these burdens and to overcome them; you who, so to speak, renewed my being twice over, doubling my fortitude, allow me to devote my pen to the task of tracing the story of your love and constancy. I shall try to excite in the hearts of my readers the emotion you inspire in me. I announce to them that it is Edmund who is going to speak.

He has so often spoken to me of his life in Texas and on Galveston Island, both in the presence of Ernestine and on our excursions beyond the confines of the camp, that after a fashion I shall make use of his own expressions, though I shall not have that fire, that enthusiasm which marked him, which animated his words, his looks, his slightest gesture. One would have to be in his place, to be consumed, as he was, by that pure true love, which moved his heart and fettered his faculties. When he uttered the name of his beloved, his voice was no longer the same, it took on an expression which startled me, and which I clearly felt, though I cannot describe the emotion it aroused.

I warn my readers that the names of Edmund and Ernestine are not those of the two colonists concerned; for I thought it more seemly to change them. But what I shall have to say is none the less strictly true.

Let us listen to Edmund:

I was in barracks at P— with my regiment. For a long time my recreation lay in careful attention to my duty and in companionship with small groups of my comrades, walking, going to plays, and readings. It chanced one day that I met a friend who was spending several days with his parents in the city where we were. I had known him in his regiment, for we had been together in barracks, and a certain similarity in disposition drew us together. We even wrote to each other frequently. He was very glad to see me, and I shared his pleasure. He made me promise to come to see him. I assured him I would certainly take advantage of his invitation; after he had given me his address we separated.

Several days passed before I was able to go to his home, for drilling and reviews prevented me, and I felt put out about it without exactly knowing why. Finally one morning I left my quarters at a suitable hour for making calls, and a cab soon took me to the neighborhood where my friend lived.

I entered a house of rather handsome exterior and was met by a servant who opened the door and showed me to the person I sought. As soon as he saw me, he came forward and reproached me for what he called my forgetfulness, for, in his opinion, I had waited too long to return his visit. I tried to excuse myself, and we went upstairs to his apartment. After we talked some time of what had happened to us both since last we met, he suggested that he introduce me to his parents, who, without actually knowing me, thought of me as their son's friend for it seems he had been rather kind in his remarks of me to them.

We then came down and found his father and mother waiting in the parlor for lunch to be announced. When my friend told them who I was, indulgent smiles and the most flattering words were their response. They invited me to have lunch with them, and I accepted. Scarcely had we seated ourselves in the dining-room when my friend's mother said to the servant in attendance:

"Will you ask my daughter to come down?" and the man left the room.

A few moments later I saw my friend's sister enter. I glanced at her, then—how can I describe what I felt? Imagine a divine being who bows with as much grace as modesty who comes to embrace her father, mother and brother, and to wish them good day in such a delightfully sweet and harmonious voice that I felt emotion take full possession of all my senses.

I had begun by doing full justice to the meal, and was most favorably disposed towards it, but suddenly my appetite disappeared; and I could no longer think of anything but of the person who had just shed into my soul a radiance which I could not as yet define.

May I try to describe Ernestine for it was by this name her mother called her in offering her some dish? Can you imagine a young woman of rich proportions, of the most regular beauty, whose complexion was far whiter than the lily and more delicately pink than the rose? She had the most beautiful eyes, and the artless arrangement of her heavy hair, coiled carelessly upon her head, but enhanced her charm; a fresh mouth, set with two rows of pearls; two small white hands which beautified everything they happened to touch. All of this gives you but a faint idea of Ernestine.

Although I was so taken with her that I could attend to nothing else, I yet hoped my attitude did not appear to be one of affectation; and when my friend urged me to eat, drawing me momentarily out of my contemplation, I continued with my food, still unable to remove my eyes from her who had become my idol, whom I loved, whom I adored with a love and admiration which she merited.

When my friend's parents asked me several questions I answered, and they seemed satisfied.

Ernestine, who up until this moment had not so much as glanced in my direction, now deliberately favored me with a look. She appeared a thousand times more beautiful.

Her mother told her to serve us, which she did; and when the time came for me to take the plate she handed me, I hastened to cover with my hand the spot her fingers had touched. I imagined that I was pressing Ernestine's hand and a delicious sensation crept over me.

Some of my readers doubtless will find me sentimental; and in truth I am, for such is my nature; it is my good fortune, and to those critics I might say: "Ah! if you had but known Ernestine."

A few words spoken by Ernestine's mother enlivened the conversation during the meal which, although fairly long, was surely drawing to a close. My friend answered his mother, the father took part, and soon we all joined in.

Ernestine gave voice to several reflections which told me her mind and her powers of discernment were consistent with her charm, and that such thoughts could not be better expressed, nor in more careful terms.

When we arose from the table, everyone was for going into the garden. I dared not offer my hand to Ernestine, but as I presented it to her mother, Ernestine's father said to her, smilingly:

"Come, my dear, let me be your escort, since neither of these young gentlemen is gallant enough to offer you his arm."

At that, as he gave her his arm, she returned his show of affection, and we all, including my friend, went into the garden.

The spot we were rambling over was indeed a delightful one. On the right I saw a little flower bed surrounded by trellises where could be seen an arbor with a plot of grass.

My friend said to me: "This is Ernestine's garden; it is

she who tends it, who waters these flowers; the roses, the violets, the mignonette; all that you see owes its freshness and its beauty to her."

I wanted to make some answer but with a lover's timidity I dared not raise my voice.

It can be imagined how delighted I was to be upon ground Ernestine so often trod, to inhale the perfume of the flowers which she herself cultivated.

We walked along the borders, and since I had a slight knowledge of botany, I could but speak of it. At this Ernestine began to question me and, oh, delight! I hastened to answer her, but not without the liveliest emotion.

How happy I was that she seemed to agree with me!

She asked us to be seated, adding with a most charming smile that she did the honors there. Taking her mother's arm she said: "Come, mother, sit in my place." I examined Ernestine's nook and saw that the branches of the rose-trees and other hedges had been rounded over her head, and that holly-hocks grew about the arbor whose beauty Ernestine was wont to enhance with her own loveliness.

I sat down on the grass which every day she set her foot upon, and I was still happier.

We were all five there, Ernestine between her parents, I next to her brother, talking of flowers which Ernestine loved so much.

She saw a pink leaning awry upon its stem and she hastened to sprinkle it. I had the opportunity to notice that the most beautiful foot also belonged to the most beautiful of women. What perfection! Oh, Ernestine! What a supernatural being you looked to my eyes.

Now today that you are mine, you are all the more so

—you are mine and I know not how to believe my good fortune! What have I done to deserve it?

After a few moments we quitted Ernestine's arbor to have a look about the garden. Soon the ladies left us to make their toilets, for they were going out.

Before leaving they bowed to us, and Ernestine's mother invited me to come to see them.

"You are my son's friend," she said to me kindly, "and so the house is open to you."

I thanked her, and they left us.

I followed Ernestine with my eyes, beholding with delight her elegant figure, and the simple white dress she wore without other ornaments. She had suppressed everything more striking. When I lost sight of her, I felt as if I could see her still.

Her brother said to me, "I am going out, my dear Edmund, and if you have no plans, won't you come with me? I have to speak with a certain person, and afterward we will walk."

I accepted, and he went to get his hat and cane.

His father said to me, "You haven't yours," and we walked in the direction of the house.

My friend was waiting. His father renewed the invitation which had already been extended to me, and I, promising to take advantage of the permission just granted, departed with the son.

When we had done our errand and paid several visits, we set out for a walk. I was dying to speak of Ernestine, but dared not as yet broach the subject, when my friend relieved my embarrassment by saying, "Well, you knew me but not my family. What do you say of my parents, how do you like my sister?"

"I can only congratulate you on belonging to them," was my answer.

"Oh, my friend, if you knew what a happy combination of goodness, virtues and lovable qualities there are combined in those dear persons whom we have just left!"

"To judge from all I have seen in my friend," I added, "there are few families which possess to a greater degree all that makes up the charm of life."

"You are right," he said, "and I am going to let you be the judge."

You can imagine with what interest I waited to hear what he was about to tell me, for necessarily Ernestine's name would come up in the conversation, and, moreover, he himself was much like her. His voice, though masculine, was much like hers, and though he was already my friend, he was to become still closer to me.

"I like to speak of my parents," he began. "You have seen my father—he is an excellent man, wise without pretense; nothing is strange to his mind, for he can discuss everything with a rare insight. He is a good husband, a good father, and twenty-five years of married life have in no wise diminished his love for my mother, who is, moreover, his friend. My sister and I are his only riches, his fortune meaning nothing to him except in so far as he can make people happy through its use. My mother is like my father; their life together is the perfect reflection of a happy day, and since I have known them, not even the smallest cloud has darkened their union. The will of one is always the desire of the other; they are an example of congeniality of disposition and spirit which it would be difficult to match.

"My sister possesses all the characteristics I admire in

39

my parents. I say nothing of her beauty, for one has only to see her to realize it; her talents and her learning are equal to her charms of which she is neither vain nor proud, and if the same blood did not course in our veins, I should have asked nothing better than to spend my life in adoring her. Fortunate a thousand and one times, my dear Edmund, the man who will prove worthy to be her husband, and who will be able to stir her heart; for although she is possessed of an exquisite sensitiveness, it will not be the matter of a moment to win her love."

What a delight it was to me to hear the one I loved, whose perfections I had already divined, so praised. My friend did not speak for a moment, though I still gave ear. We went on a few steps in a silence which I finally broke in fear and embarrassment.

"Your sister, my friend, must be the object of universal desires and reverence; has she, perhaps, made her choice?"

"No! My parents, who are rather hard to please when it comes to choosing their friends, have casual acquaintances and go in society, but are intimate with no one; besides, my mother is my sister's closest friend; they are inseparable. If an unfamiliar sentiment were to move her heart, I am sure she would have no other confidant than her and my father, who idolizes his daughter. They love her more than they do me, though the tenderness of my parents for their son is marked; she merits this preference, and I am not jealous of it. Besides how could one dare be envious of Ernestine? How could one dare to compare himself to my good, my excellent, my wonderful sister?"

"You are right," I said in tones of enthusiasm. "How fortunate you are to be her brother, to see her every hour!"

"Heavens!" he said smiling to me, "How you do take fire, dear Edmund!" and he regarded me intently. "Don't go falling in love with my sister, for I cannot answer for her undertaking your cure; yet I do not wonder that you should, since you have seen her."

Our walk was at an end, for he was to return to his parents, and when we parted he made me promise to come back to see them.

"You have been invited by everyone; come, and I shall always find a new pleasure in being with you."

He pressed my hand and turned away. I followed him with my glance, finding something of Ernestine in the whole of his person; but I soon lost sight of him and felt myself alone in the world.

I abandoned myself to my dreams, Ernestine alone occupying my thoughts: retracing in memory all that her brother had told me of her, all that I had seen myself, I made vows and gave myself up to desires which doubtless were foolish but the land of dreams is the domain of lovers and poets. I returned home absorbed in these reflections. When night came I could not resist the temptation to draw near to Ernestine, that I might breathe the same air with her. I changed my clothes, put on a coat, pulled my round hat down over my eyes, and sped to the neighborhood where Ernestine dwelled.

Everything was calm and peaceful as I approachad her house with darkness favoring me. The shutters were closed, and I stationed myself opposite against the wall where I could see lights in the rooms. Soon the sound of a harp was heard, playing a prelude, and then a voice, as sweet as it was melodious, intoned some words I could not distinguish.

But my beating heart told me without doubt that it was Ernestine who was singing and accompanying herself, and I stayed until I no longer heard anything. Then I returned to my lodging, more smitten than ever, wishing passionately for the dawn of day, that I might go back to be near Ernestine once more.

I passed the night a victim to the most violent agitation, for sleep flies from lovers. Finally, when day-break began to chase away the shadows of night, I prepared to go out, and I was ready a great while before I heard the ringing of the bell which marks the hour when it is permissible to call. This hour, so much desired, rang out on the air, and I left, guided by love and hope. I was intoxicated at the thought of seeing Ernestine. I reached my destination; but suddenly something, I knew not what stayed me. I reflected: though they have invited me to come back, to appear the very day following might not be exactly the thing; I might displease them; and at this thought I retraced my steps. Twenty times was I on the point of conquering this false pride, this timidity and twenty times did I resist the desire, while a secret voice said to me: "Go, and thou wilt find happiness." I spent the whole day in that state of uncertainty and anxiety, and evening found me still undecided. I did not see Ernestine.

The next day brought the same torments. I was undecided as to what I should do, when I received a letter from my friend, reproaching me for failing to avail myself of the invitation which had been extended me, but telling me that nevertheless I was expected for lunch, and that, if I foresaw no active service during the next two days, I must spend the time with his family in the country. I leaped for joy when I read that precious note, and went to the colonel to ask him for two days' leave. I secured it and flew at once to Ernestine on wings of love and hope.

When I arrived, they reproached me in the most pleasing manner, and I tried to excuse myself without divulging my real reason; but my friend guessed it and smiled. My eyes were seeking for Ernestine. Her brother said maliciously: "I wish to announce Ernestine to you." She in fact did come in, a straw hat dangling in her hand. Heavens! but she was beautiful! I bowed to her, spoke to her. She answered artlessly, without affectation, that they had been expecting me, while she petted a little dog which seemed very dear to her. I stammered out a few insignificant words, for one is so stupid when one is in love. Ernestine looked at me a moment, then turning to her mother, asked her what was the hour fixed for our departure.

"After lunch, my dear," was the answer.

We sat down at the table to a short meal. It was announced that the horses were in the carriage, and we went down. We set out with the ladies inside, the father and I in front, and my friend on horseback. What good fortune! I found myself opposite Ernestine. I could look at her to my heart's content.

Her hat, adorned with but a simple ribbon knotted under her chin, made her face more strikingly lovely. The little dog, which was one of the party, climbed into my lap, and although they wanted to drive him off, I begged them to leave him, since he was Ernestine's.

I was happy.

The various scenes which presented themselves to our eyes were the topic of conversation. The subject of drawing came up, and, since I was possessed of a certain amount

43

of talent, I spoke of it not badly, I believe, I saw my three travelling companions smile, without understanding why. As we were going at a lively clip, we were not long in reaching our destination. Ernestine, light as air, jumped quickly down. Two young children came to embrace her, and we went into the house.

My friend had gone ahead, and we found ourselves in a pretty parlor whose simplicity was its greatest charm. Some framed drawings of very fine execution, constituted the decoration, and on examining them, I recognized the various scenes along our road to the house. Only then did I divine the cause for the smiles, and I suspected at once that the drawings were Ernestine's work. Why had I not guessed? Had her brother not told me that she was possessed of every talent?

He now aroused me from my observations by inviting me to make a tour of the house. We went over all the apartments while Ernestine was with her mother, who was giving orders, and seemed much gayer than in town. We found them downstairs, and Ernestine came playfully up, asking me if I played with my sister, to which I replied that I had none.

"Oh, that is a shame," she said.

"Yes, but I should like to have one, if she were like you."

"How gallant you are, M. Edmund; that is fine," and she turned away, my heart following her.

I believed myself transported into another world. I could see Ernestine and was privileged to spend two days with her, during which I said to myself, "Ah, if they could but go on forever." But happy hours hurry past.

I sought her out ceaselessly, wishing to secure command

44

of my desire, my glances, and my impatience. Her brother who was with me, and who was of a happy disposition, observed me with a sly smile, as I everywhere looked for Ernestine's things, or an object she might have made. A piano had been placed in the parlor, and upon it there was a sonata with a violin accompaniment which she had copied. I sat down to the instrument and played the prelude. Ernestine came up to me.

"Ah, M. Edmund, you are a musician," she said at once. "How delightful! You shall soon accompany me, if you but will. Go on!"

It was the first time Ernestine had spoken to me in such a direct fashion, and I felt the strongest, yet the sweetest emotion. I did not lose my head, however, and went on with the piece. I do not know whether it was that love came to my aid, or that I was galvanized by Ernestine, but never did any violin bring forth such sounds from beneath the bow. Ernestine's father and mother came into the parlor, but I was unaware of their presence until a bravo of applause resounded when I had finished playing the piece. I was complimented on what they were pleased to call my talent, and it was agreed that in the evening we should have some more music. As we left the room my friend said to me, "Let's go for a walk."

Ernestine, who remained with her parents, smiled when she saw us leaving, and added, "We will have the music soon." My answer was a nod. I was too greatly agitated to speak a word, and I had to content myself with allowing my glance to dwell for a moment upon the idol of my heart.

We crossed the garden and soon found ourselves in the open country. Ernestine's brother began the conversation.

"I did not know you were a musician, my dear Edmund; it is a desirable talent, and a great resource in all the circumstances of life; for music makes solitude more beautiful, and in society it is both useful and pleasant. Better still, it reveals amiability, which goes with good morals and regular conduct. You played that prelude a little while ago with expression which would do credit to a consumate artist." He looked at me as he spoke, "Your instrument appeared to live and breathe beneath your fingers; you seemed really inspired."

He smiled knowingly, and I began to be embarrassed, but I took myself in hand and answered him, "Music is one of the accomplishments for which I have a taste, and which I have cultivated with care. I have been a soldier for a long time, and it, together with reading, are becoming my only diversions. I do not care for noisy pleasures, and still less for gaming; I associate with my comrades without being intimate with any, for I rather like being alone; my violin and my books afford me some delightful moments. When I am with them, I am never bored."

"You would get on well with us: my family has tastes similar to yours; my sister is an excellent musician and sings charmingly. If you were but to hear her at the harp or piano you would be astonished; such harmonious expression and brilliant technique are rare. You will soon know for yourself, and I am persuaded that you will not be sorry to accompany Ernestine. What do you say to it?"

"I shall be very flattered."

"I think so."

His glance followed me and his eyes questioned mine. I wanted to appear at ease, but I was disturbed.

46

"My dear Edmund," he added, "you are trying to hide your feelings; I am going to confide in you: It is not for nothing that you have seen my sister, and I am not surprised at this, for such has been the story of all those who approach her; but the effect on you, I see, has been real and lasting. Your emotion is still too new to be a menace to your reason; I would advise you to use this reason, for I know my sister well enough to be sure that she will not easily share the feeling she may inspire. With her it is respect that will give birth to love. Please do not feel, dear Edmund, that I do not think you worthy of inspiring both; on the contrary, but the path is stormy for him who would win my sister. I would not so far do you an injustice as to suspect you of being capable of employing other means than those allowable to a man of delicate honor. No, you are my friend, and that name tells you enough of what I think of you. But since you love my sister, I am sure that the two days you will spend with us will not be without danger for you. But after all, it is your own affair."

I replied, "You must know, my friend, that what you have just said embarrasses me. But I must speak to you frankly, for such is the need, the desire of my heart. Yes, I love your beautiful Ernestine and I feel that it is forever."

He laughingly interrupted me.

"Lover's words, my dear Edmund. Remember that this fire which consumes you, as it has so many others, is too violent not to die more or less quickly; for, in general, it doesn't last long."

"You do your sister an injustice; when one really loves her, it must be for life."

"I grant you that she may be an exception to the rule, and

47

that you, knowing and appreciating her, may not easily change; but, after all, we are both men; love is, they say, a weakness, which may be destroyed by another weakness."

"When one loves Ernestine, it is a virtue, and I, for my part, can tell you that when one possesses this virtue it but grows stronger with the passing days."

"That last word forces me to hold my peace, my dear Edmund. I am conquered, and acknowledge my defeat. Do not forget this expression, much less the fact, for it can be useful to you. Does one know? A tender tie goes further than one might think. But let's return; we have been gone for a long time."

I could ask nothing better, for I was going to see Ernestine again. We began speaking of other things, and were soon back.

The first person I saw was Ernestine. This meeting appeared to me in the light of a happy augury, particularly as I now found her prettier and more charming than ever, and was hourly discovering new beauties in her. I divined many precious qualities: but time alone could show me, could make me appreciate her judgment, her mentality, and the strength of her mind. She reproached us for our too-prolonged absence and said, "Gentlemen, you should not leave the company so when you are in the country. Such behavior is to be reproved. At any rate, dear brother, I see your influence there, for you are always having to run up hill and down dale."

"It was a pleasure to show Edmund the country surrounding our home, and then we gossiped about some very interesting things."

"And about what, gentlemen, if you please?"

"Oh, about the beauties of—nature."

"That does not surprise me; Edmund is well up in botany."

With any other man than my friend, than Ernestine's brother, I would have been afraid of an indiscretion, but he respected his sister too much, he respected himself too much, to forget the consideration he owed her, and which I myself had a right to expect of him.

Ernestine asked me what I thought of the landscape I had seen.

"Very pretty, very interesting; the views are varied and picturesque; and I would willingly spend my life here."

The conversation went no further.

M. and Madame Dormeuil came in—for this was the name of Ernestine's parents.

"Ah, here are our travelers," said M. Dormeuil. "You are exercising very early in the morning, gentlemen. I heartily approve, and at your age I would have done the same thing. Today although I am at liberty to stretch my legs, I am a little more of a stay-at-home. I confine my walks to my garden or to short rambles in the country. When we wish to visit some neighbors, we all go together, Madame and I and dear Ernestine; but her small delicate foot suffers somewhat from the hard earth. Fortunately, she will never have to travel on foot, at least; isn't that true, daughter?"

"Yes, dear papa," she said, and a kiss ended the sentence.

"Mademoiselle," added I, in my turn, "will never go on any long voyage?"

"Not without fear, for I should not like the ocean. But, after all, I am wrong to talk this way, for one should not fear what one does not know, and, moreover, one has to take circumstances into account and to know at need how to face the storm."

Madame Dormeuil looked at her daughter. As for me, I admired her: the freshest of mouths had just opened to give expression and sound to a reasoned observation.

Madame Dormeuil turned laughingly to me: "My daughter is the stuff heroines are made of, and she would become one if need be."

"Why not, Mama," returned Ernestine, "do you think me spineless and without energy? Be kinder to yourself, as well as to my good father; I am your child and I can and must be like you."

"That's all very well, sister," added the younger Dormeuil; "let it go at that. I can judge you much better; and I think you are capable of doing all that is kind, gentle, generous, even extraordinary."

"Dear brother, that is too much, that is exaggeration, flattery—but I forgive you for it. M. Edmund, don't take all that seriously. I am far from being a prodigy."

"I think, Mademoiselle, that the picture is not a flattering one."

There was quiet at this, and I added nothing more. Oh, Ernestine! You were too modest, and I did not yet know how to appreciate you. How far you were above all the praise heaped upon you, you did not yourself know.

The younger Dormeuil changed the subject by reminding us that we were to play, and that I was to accompany Ernestine, an idea which met with the approval of the father. I took up the violin, Ernestine seated herself at the piano, and we began. It was a sonata of one of our great masters, and Ernestine performed it with marked superiority, while I had the good fortune to accompany her in a way that called forth praise.

"Very fine, M. Edmund," with charming grace, "just think what it would have been if you had studied this sonata. Oh, we shall practice together which will have the added advantage of giving my parents some pleasant moments, for they both love and understand music."

I assured Ernestine that I would try to follow her, and I accepted her proposal to play several variations, being delighted to see that she surpassed all her brother had said. I begged her to sing, and she charmingly complied with modesty and real talent. My violin blended with the pathos of her pure and melodious voice; and in a mirror which was opposite the piano I could see reflected her angelic countenance. Oh, Ernestine, when you sang those verses on friendship, you made them divine by the expression you put into the words; your soul imparted a new life to the thought, to the language of the gods. What would it have been like if you had sung of love?

I believed myself transported into another world, an illusion to which Ernestine gave the charm of reality. What happiness! No alien thought came near to trouble her, and my heart, my love, my rapture were as pure as was she who was the object of my homage and my secret desires, and I knew that until this moment, I had not existed. Ernestine changed everything, and I became a new being. I immediately conceived the desire to be worthy of her, to rid myself of all my faults, and to try to please her was to make a resolution to become better.

We had music several times during those two days; we talked of literature, of science and art. M. Dormeuil spoke familiarly of all, and Madame Dormeuil showed herself worthy of being Ernestine's mother. Hers was the most refined taste, hers the most delicate tact, and the purest utterances. The choicest words came naturally to her lips, and her manner agreed with all else. The most regular handwriting completed the list. The younger Dormeuil possessed merits and much learning, but his sister was a dangerous rival for him.

Those sweet moments, which I never would have wanted to see an end to, sped by. We returned to P—, and when they invited me to spend the rest of the day with them, I begged their permission to show myself to the Colonel in order to prove that I had not overstayed the leave so graciously granted me. When I presented myself, he received me kindly, for I had won his esteem by my faithfulness in the performance of duty.

After having spoken to him of what was pertinent to my office, I retired, went home to change my clothes, and was soon at M. Dormeuil's house, where they thanked me for my promptness, and before long we all sat down at the table. My love, already great, was growing with each instant. Oh, you who have been in love, have pity on me, for I had not yet dared speak of it! I had no confidant other than my heart, of whose state you may easily judge. After the dinner, which was rather prolonged, we went into the salon, M. and Madame Dormeuil and Ernestine going on into another room; and when the son proposed that we go down into the garden to take the air, I accepted with alacrity. Scarcely had we found ourselves there when he began speaking to me in this wise:

"Do you know, my dear Edmund, that you are creating a sensation here? I am really flattered, because I am convinced that you deserve it. My parents are pleased with you, and have congratulated me upon having made your acquaintance.

Even my sister speaks well of you; and she can do so without apprehension, since she is in agreement with my parents. This is not a bad augury for your suit, and how can one tell? In time people end by knowing each other better, and . . ."

I interrupted him, "Oh, my dear friend, do not go on, do not encourage me with a hope which, though I yield myself to it, may never be realized! I am in love with, I adore, I idolize your sister; I do not dare to fathom, to look into the future. I am, however, abandoning myself to the feeling which leads me. How would it be then if I dreamed that such a great happiness could fall to my lot? My dear Dormeuil, have pity on the emotion to which you see me a victim. You must condone and pardon me, for Ernestine is the cause of it. What would I not do in order to be worthy of her choice! I would give half of my life to be able to devote the remainder to her."

At the same time I was firmly grasping my friend's hand, and was speaking with an emotion and a fire which astonished him, and which threw him into a silence that he finally broke, saying "Calm yourself, get over this upset; your very features are altered, your voice changed. Let us go as far as the end of the garden, we will return directly, and I advise you to go to your room a few moments, for you need to be alone; and believe me, my friend, that if I speak thus to you it is for your own good. If one day my parents and Ernestine must know of your feelings, you will grant that at present they are ignorant of them. As for me, rest assured your secret lies buried in my heart, and that the friendship I bear you will be the seal of its safety. Tomorrow morning at eight o'clock, I shall be in your quarters. Now come, tell all the family goodnight."

We went back into the parlor where the ladies were reading; M. Dormeuil was taking a walk. They spied us and said: "Ah, there you are, gentlemen, you must have secrets to tell each other, you seem so to love being together, all right, all right!"

When I spoke of leaving them, they renewed their invitation to me, not a general one, but for every day, saying my place would aways be set, and that I knew their meal hours, which was all that was necessary. I thanked them for a kindness, whose whole graciousness I understood, by assuring them I should try to be worthy. I was told that I had nothing to do to make myself so. When I bowed to the ladies and M. Dormeuil, Ernestine raised her beautiful eyes to mine and said, " 'Till tomorrow then." Her brother ushered me to the door and I returned home.

"What! I shall see her every day!" I said to myself as I walked along, and I repeated it a hundred times before I reached my lodgings. Once there, I thought of all I had to fear or hope for. I loved for always, but did Ernestine share my passion? And, would her parents resign her to me? Her brother, it is true, was my friend.

Immediately a terrible and cruel thought came to tear at my heart and deprive me of all hope, for, I said, "He *seems* to be interested in me; but it is perhaps only through a sort of pity, a sort of humoring of a sick person, that he has lent an ear to my love. I shall see him tomorrow, and what will he have to say to me?" What a problem! I wanted to be with him, yet I dreaded his very presence. It was in this ebb and flow of ideas that the hours dragged past. Oh, love, how sweet are all thy pleasures: but how bitter are thy pains, how cruel thy torments! To make matters worse, Dormeuil

54

kept me waiting. When he knocked I let him in and scanned his face to divine if he were going to tell me something disastrous; his greeting reassured me.

"Well, dear Edmund, how is your heart?" was his first question. "If your face is any indication, you did not sleep very well. Just think, you have known my sister only a few days, and already you are developing symptoms of real love; how on earth would it be if you had been in love for several years?—you would succumb. You assuredly do not, as yet, have to be sorry for yourself; if the one you love has promised you nothing, she at least has not refused you. I have not come to console you, my friend, to tell you to possess your soul in patience, that you will end by ruining your beauty. Neither do you hear me flattering you. You are thought of in my family, I am sure, only as an honest man who is good company; moreover no one at home has spoken to me of you, and I have been careful not to say a single word. You will come to see us today—perhaps each passing hour will better your position. Oh, I know that lovers are not very patient; that they are quick to take alarm; but also it takes but little to calm their fears. I suggest then that you get more of a hold on yourself, and though my sister, above all women, deserves to be loved, that is no reason for losing your head. What would they think of you if it was known that you are so weak? Friendship is forgiving, you know, and I shall bury in forgetfulness what I have just been a witness to. If Ernestine were to learn of it, you would certainly have no success with her. Come, my dear Edmund, be a man, and try to conquer your love—virtuous as it may be—even though she who inspires it is entirely worthy."

I had listened to Dormeuil without interrupting him, for

I felt the justice of his remarks. I was in love with Ernestine, and I thought I was right, without, however, being able to blame him.

"Thank you for your advice, my dear Dormeuil; it springs from interest and the sincerest attachment, and I must answer by explaining myself frankly; in opening my heart to you without reserve. I love your sister, you know, and henceforth nothing can change me, whatever my fate may be. To be happy, to attain the only blessing I desire, I shall use only such means as you yourself may indicate. You are my friend—now be my aide. I do not ask you to help me; I know that before I dare raise my eyes to Ernestine to speak to her of love, I must have her parents and her own permission; if I win it, I have nothing else to ask; if it is refused me, I shall, at least, have nothing to reproach myself for. I should, doubtless, in that event, complain of my destiny; but I would be at peace with honor, and so less unhappy!"

Dormeuil answered quickly: "One who holds such sentiments deserves happiness. Speak to my parents, to my sister, let them know you. Everything leads me to believe you will not be repulsed, and if you are favorably received, you may be certain that I shall do all within my power for you, considering all interests. Think about all that, dear Edmund; take several days to be sure that you are making progress in the minds of Ernestine and my parents; use the resources of your mind to please them; follow the impulses of your honest heart, which will not lead you astray. That is enough on that score. If you have nothing better to do, dress, and we will go out; and while you are waiting for the hour when you can come to the house, we will take a walk."

I accepted the offer, was quickly ready, and we set out. We met several officers of the regiment, who went along with us. In due time we separated, and my friend and I were soon in the house which had become my universe.

I was received as usual. I thought, however, I noticed more freedom, more cordiality in my welcome; Ernestine herself treated me with less indifference and said, when she saw me with her brother: "There are the two inseparables." Then, assuming a little pout, which made her still prettier, she reproached her brother for his neglect since I had been coming to the house, threatening that she would be angry with him if it continued.

I answered that I could not forgive myself if I had been the cause of such a misfortune.

"Do not worry, my dear Edmund," Dormeuil said to me. "It would be the first time in her life for Ernestine to exhibit anger. You do not know her as yet, and besides, it is easy to judge for yourself if it is possible that such features can show anything but goodness of heart."

I approved my friend's judgment. M. and Madame Dormeuil smiled, and Ernestine said to her brother: "Will you hush? Sir, you know I do not like praise; besides, you make me blush at your words, and M. Edmund would end by accusing you of partiality."

I wanted to reply to this, but Ernestine got up and said: "We should never finish with this, and I am not sorry that luncheon will end this conversation."

When M. and Madame Dormeuil followed Ernestine, we all did likewise, and by chance, I found myself beside my idol. They treated me as if I were a member of the household.

"Make yourself at home," M. Dormeuil said to me, "for you are, so to speak, our regular guest," at which a little dialogue sprang up between us.

"I do not know how to accept such kindness."

"From the very first you inspired the greatest confidence in us; and, besides, your intimacy with my son, who is very hard to please in the choice of his friends and acquaintances, put me entirely at rest, for you must know that we do not open our doors to everyone. We know how to be content with each other, and strangers are not necessary to us. You have proved an exception to the rule, M. Edmund, as you know, and I foresee that we shall have reason to congratulate ourselves on a preference which you deserve."

"I shall try to justify that good opinion. Everything urges me that way and makes it a duty."

"Are your parents still living?"

At this question, an expression of pain must have crossed my face, and altered it perceptibly.

"What's the matter?" asked Ernestine.

"Nothing, Mademoiselle. Your father has just reminded me of what I lost in my parents, and I am sad."

"A cruel thing it is, not to be able to embrace one's parents every day."

M. Dormeuil was quick to say: "I am indeed sorry to have revived your grief; but it does you honor, and I am persuaded that you were a good son, and with that precious quality, one always has many others. How old are you, sir?"

"Twenty-eight."

"You should think of marrying, for I am sure that you would make your wife happy."

"I intend to follow my father's example. To form those

bonds, a man must find the right woman, and often the one upon whom we look with love, who attracts and deserves our choice, cannot belong to us. It is much easier to love than to be loved."

"I am aware of that, but you have all that is necessary to your success. What is your fortune?"

"Forty thousand francs income."

"That can smooth out money difficulties."

"Yes, sir, but that is not all; when one consults only the material side, happiness is not always present."

I was not displeased that M. Dormeuil had brought this subject up, and I saw that everyone was very attentive. Ernestine had a certain preoccupied air, and the younger Dormeuil looked at me half serious, half smiling, with a glance whose import only I could fathom.

M. Dormeuil went on: "Your observation is true; but when one is independent, one may find something that imparts a new value to his independence; and in the class of society in which you move, where you must look for a wife, there are young women who will make excellent mothers of families and most respectable wives."

"Certainly," added Madame Dormeuil, who until that moment had said nothing.

"Besides, sir," I went on, "for me to think of marriage would perhaps be unwise, for I am a soldier of rank, and since I have chosen the career of arms, I must follow it. I should have to leave my wife; and, in the event of war breaking out again, such a separation would expose her to the cruellest uncertainties."

"Every calling has its advantages and disadvantages," said M. Dormeuil. "All that is compensated for in the life one leads. It is true that soldiers run great dangers; but it is also true that glory has its charms, for it elevates the soul and is a valuable incentive to men, and, upon my word, one does well to make sacrifices to it. Then, it must be admitted that women love warriors, for they have as much strength and courage as we have. And love of the kind a man would inspire in a woman must always give heed to the voice of honor; she would never counsel the one she loves to anything which might reflect upon honor. It must be said in their favor that women are perfect in this respect; they will always find in me a partisan and an apologist, for I am their knight against everything. Isn't that true, Ernestine?"

"Yes, Papa," she answered, "and I do not regret it."

"I am always right, with you."

"Consequently you are a spoiled child, very spoiled," said her brother, "but you deserve to be. Edmund, don't think she has taken advantage of the weakness we have for her. She is, really, next to my mother, the best of women; and if I were not her brother, I would have accomplished the impossible in order to become her husband."

I was bold enough to add: "Many men would be of the same mind, but that is a good fortune to which not everyone can aspire."

Dormeuil answered: "Not everyone, no; but men can be found who are worthy of this preference."

Ernestine, looking at both of us and smiling with infinite charm, said: "Gentlemen, will you please stop concerning yourselves with my marriage. If by chance someone sets eyes on me who is so inclined, he will speak of it, and I shall know it; if I like him, I will call my little council together, and we will then come to a decision. If you will hear me, let's have done with this and go into the parlor. I want to have music. I received some new pieces yesterday which I should like to try, and if M. Edmund is willing we shall attempt them."

"Mademoiselle, never was there anything more agreeable."

Everyone rose, and M. Dormeuil, clapping me on the shoulder, said: "Come, my friend—for I regard you as such —come play the violin while you are awaiting your marriage."

Everything was soon arranged. The music we were to try was Italian, by one of the best composers. Ernestine began; her light fingers, scarcely touching the keys, drew from the piano harmonies that sank into the soul. The instrument I had was excellent, and I commenced a solo, at which I surpassed myself. I was a changed mortal, for I was near Ernestine and could see her. When I finished, she said to me, "Ah, M. Edmund, how well you played that! Again please."

"Yes, again, again!" repeated the gallery.

I began again, Ernestine following with her eyes the movement of my bow. She, being an excellent musician, understood its different positions. I finished and let my hand fall.

"That's delightful," said she, taking mine in her own. I seized her beautiful hand, and raising it a little, I said, bending low: "Do you permit me, Mademoiselle?"

M. Dormeuil did not give her time to answer, "Yes, the *encore* merits that favor."

I pressed her hand with my lips, and I thought she trembled slightly. O, sweet and unlooked-for happiness, how precious thou wast to me! The memory of thee still makes my heart beat faster. There are impressions which time cannot efface.

Ernestine, I have been your husband for a long time, and I still experience those delightful sensations, for they are as real as at the moment I have just described.

I was asked if I had any voice, to which I answered, "A little." The younger Dormeuil got up and, looking about in his sister's music, drew out *The Timid Lover*, which he put on the rack. I could not retreat now, and as I glanced over the melody, Ernestine said she would accompany me.

"You will lend my voice a charm which otherwise it does not possess." But my friend interrupted with, "Come, modest singer, begin!" And without appearing to do so intentionally, I sought to portray the fears and confusion of a lover who does not make an avowal, yet loves madly.

"That is very good; it is astonishing. You sing with a deal of taste," said M. and Madame Dormeuil.

"Ah! I made you a real present when I introduced Edmund to you, and you will thank me for it one day; you do not really know him as yet, for he has merit and you will see that he will get along in life," and he laughed.

Ernestine thoughtfully strummed a few notes on the piano, as if far away; M. and Madame Dormeuil complimented me, while I regarded in the mirror the reflection of Ernestine's lovely face. She arose, and glancing about with a look that seemed to take in the situation, went up to her mother and said, "Mama, let's go down into the garden," and we left.

As for me, my heart was aflame from the contact of my lips with Ernestine's hand. Once in the garden the flowers and the hedges occupied our attention. There was at the bottom, a little summer-house which I had not seen; it was Ernestine's work-room, and when we went in I found the walls fairly covered with pictures. I noticed her portrait drawn by herself, as well as those of her parents in which the resemblance was striking; all were of a delectable fineness.

"Do you draw, M. Edmund?" she said to me, while my eyes were fixed on her adored likeness.

"Yes, Mademoiselle, a little."

"Let's see what he can do," said the younger Dormeuil.

"Yes, let's," added the father; and, although I protested, they put a pencil in my hand, and I sat down. There was paper beneath my fingers, and the portrait of Ernestine before my eyes. I seized at once the opportunity and sketched in the features which were already engraved upon my heart. Love steadied my hand, guided my pencil; and the eyes fixed upon me soon saw a striking likeness.

"In truth, my dear Edmund, you can do anything," the father said to me. "Ernestine, what do you say to his work?"

At this I rose and offered it to her. She took it, blushing a little.

"Thank you, it is very good; but you might have chosen another model."

"Ah, Mademoiselle," I replied, "what other could have been worthy of the choice, I ask you." And everyone, laughing, agreed with me.

I should have much liked to keep the precious sketch, but that would have been an indiscretion, and I did not even ask it as I watched Ernestine roll it up and hold it in her hand.

We left the summer-house and continued our walk in the garden, I near to M. Dormeuil, who addressed me.

"I see with pleasure, M. Edmund, that you are possessed of talents and knowledge; they are the fruits of your love

63

for the arts and sciences, and prove, to your credit, that you did not consume your youth in futile occupations and dissipation. I am astonished that you should have attained to such a degree of perfection, since you are a soldier."

"Sir, the arts and sciences always held an irresistible attraction for me; and, as such pursuits leave in their wake neither regrets nor remorse, I abandoned myself entirely to them."

Ernestine did not speak; but as she walked I admired the elegance and grace of her body, her foot which seemed scarcely to press the earth, for in vain did I seek the imprint of her steps. Each instant I discovered a new charm in the object of my love which thus, to my delight, became more violent. When we reached her borders, she stepped in, pulled some flowers and made a bouquet of them. Her brother asked her for a rose, which she gave him, fastening it in his buttonhole.

"Everyone must have a flower," he said to her, and she gave one to her father, her mother and, at last, to me. How happy I was! I possessed something that had been hers. I thanked her, and we returned to the house, speaking of an afternoon jaunt which I was to join. M. and Madame Dormeuil and Ernestine were to go in the carriage; Dormeuil and I would ride horseback; thus the party was arranged to the satisfaction of all. I had to return to my quarters for my spurs, and my friend went with me so that I would be back more promptly. I was not sorry of his company, since I had so many things to tell him. I bowed to the ladies and we went out.

"My friend, your sister has made such an impression on me that I love her to the point where my happiness and my very existence are bound up in that sentiment. Give me your opinion; I intend to speak to your parents about it, and so have the goodness to warn them, to beg them to grant me a moment's interview. I think such are the preliminary steps in order to reach your sister; what do you think of them?"

"You are right, my friend; but I will say to my parents only that you wish to speak to them about a matter, and will not tell them what you have to say; for otherwise they would ask me questions, which, if I appeared to know more, would embarrass me, and besides, the more discreet you are, the more grateful will my parents and even Ernestine be to you for such attentions and the refinement of your demeanor. Do not worry; they will hear you, and I wish you the success you desire."

Do you think they will listen to me with favor?"

"I could not say; but judging by the esteem they have for you, I think you may hope; the results will tell if I guess aright."

We reached my quarters, where I quickly changed my clothes, and on our return we found everything ready, and were soon in the open fields, we on horseback and they in the carriage. I rode a very pretty horse which jumped spirit-edly several times, and when he tried to rear, I mastered him with difficulty, drawing a word of praise from Dor-meuil. We rode, one on each side of the carriage, and Dor-meuil in a very gay mood made us laugh, so that we were all soon in the humor, and agreeable talk and pleasantries were the burden of the conversation. I, in enchantment, could see Ernestine, who laughed at our silly actions and words, for we were spurred on still further by the most beautiful weather imaginable. What a happy day! What de-

65

lightful moments! All had lately been so for me, and might become even happier. I desired, yet dreaded, the interview I had solicited, which was to take place on our return.

We did not proceed very rapidly, our horses being put at a slow trot so we could chatter at our ease as we rode along. We saw a little town in the distance; Dormeuil's proposal that we make a stop there was approved, and we were not long in reaching it. We got down, watered the horses, and moved over to the banks of the river but a short distance away. My friend took his mother's arm while I remained with M. Dormeuil and Ernestine. We were a little way from each other, and I suspected that Dormeuil would take advantage of the moment to make of his mother the request with which I had charged him. When we came up they were laughing, and Madame Dormeuil looked at me with a certain curiosity. We had to return to Paris, she said, and I imagined that I had something to do with this departure, which was more hurried than had been planned. We retraced our steps and were soon on our way home. The return was more quiet, for each was occupied with his own thoughts. As we rode along, Dormeuil told me that as soon as we returned, I could speak to his mother, who had questioned him; but he had been reserved, insisting that he was absolutely ignorant of what I had to say. The nearer we approached to Paris, the more uneasy I became, and I looked at Ernestine, saying to myself, "What if I might possess entirely the most perfect thing that nature has formed! Ah, if I can win her, my happiness will exceed my hopes, and I shall have nothing left to live for; my whole life will be too little to insure the happiness of the most beloved of women."

I resolved to steel myself, for I might be refused, even

though there was no real objection to me. Dormeuil, who was at my side, said to me: "You seem very preoccupied."

"Are you surprised at that? I am flying in the face of events that, in an hour perhaps, will decide my fate, and I shall be the most unfortunate or the happiest of men."

"Come, courage! A man, above all a soldier, should be ready for anything."

We were entering the city and our talk ceased. We arrived before M. Dormeuil's door, the carriage entered the yard, and we were soon in the parlor.

I noticed Madame Dormeuil leave the room. An instant later a servant came to say that she wished to speak to me, and, on following him, I found myself in her company. She saved me the embarrassment of speaking first, saying to me, smiling: "My son told me you wished to speak to me, M. Edmund. Tell me what I can do for you, and, if I consult only the friendship that you have inspired in me, all will be easy."

Although this beginning encouraged me, I experienced a rising emotion which she did not fail to notice.

"How now, it's really serious, then! You are trembling all over, but calm yourself and speak out. There is nothing in me which should frighten you."

I then broached the subject.

"Madame, the way you have received me into your house has been truly flattering, and you have inspired me with respect and gratitude. I could not see her, who, besides yourself, is its chief ornament, without a lively and sincere sentiment. I love Mademoiselle Ernestine, and my happiness would be to tell her so, and to prove it to her. I have deemed it best to speak first to you, to obtain your views;

67

and if they are not unfavorable, I might dare hope one day to be attached to you by the tenderest and most sacred of ties."

"Your request does me honor, M. Edmund, and the straightforwardness and consideration of your actions on this occasion but adds to the good opinion I already had of you. If I have a certain authority over my daughter, it does not go so far as to try to rule her heart. I believe she could not choose better, but before giving you the slightest hope, I must speak to her, as well as to M. Dormeuil, of your intentions. It is saying enough to you that I do not refuse you. Be discreet, and in a few days, sooner perhaps, you will know how the matter stands. Let us return to the others."

I thanked her for her kindnesses.

"Well, now," she went on, "how could I do other than approve of you, my friend?"

"Ah! madame, if it can only be that ere long you may give me another name!"

"I am aware of all the desire you may have for this other name, but patience was never a lover's virtue; come." And we returned to the parlor.

M. Dormeuil was alone, book in hand.

"Where do you two come from?"

"We had something to say to each other."

"All right, I am not curious."

The remainder of the day passed easily, and all that was said was of the greatest interest to me. Ernestine was still charming, but how could I have found her otherwise; each instant showed her more lovable, more attractive in my eyes.

I was forgetting that I should be gone when the striking

hour reminded me. I begged them to pardon my indiscretion.

"Oh, there is no harm," said Madame Dormeuil with a very expressive smile.

"What can one do, Madame? Everything here takes me out of myself and holds me. I can well believe I am in my own home, so thoroughly do you seem to forget with pleasure that it is yours. I ask your pardon, a thousand times."

"You are not guilty—tomorrow then."

I left the room and came up with young Dormeuil.

"Well, did you speak to my mother?"

"Yes, nothing is decided yet."

"I imagine."

"If I have no definite hope, at least I did not elicit a refusal."

"I understand that, too."

"I shall have an answer in a few days, perhaps tomorrow."

"Will you come?"

"Certainly, for I am a prey to mortal dreads."

"That does not surprise me. Poor lover, I pity you. Do not come too early, but wait for me. I will come to fetch you, at which time I may, perhaps, be able to tell you some good news. Well, off with you now."

I left him. It would seem that he divined my impatience, for early the next day I saw him coming. He did not give me time to question him.

"My dear Edmund, when I had not even intended coming, they sent me. My mother acquainted father with your request, who approved it, if Ernestine is willing. She was consulted and feels no repugnance, but has not yet given an answer. Your behaviour, however, has flattered her, and she appreciates your having spoken to my mother before making your love known to her. That action has disposed

69

her in your favor. Perhaps it may interest you to know that. But at any rate, come with me right away."

I danced with joy, and ran madly about, or rather, flew.

I was soon at M. Dormeuil's, and when I went in I found him with his wife; Ernestine was in her room, and I was received with pleasant laughter.

"Come, my friend," the father said to me, "you wish to become our son, and we desire it too, because you seem to us worthy of the treasure we would entrust to you, and if she consents, you shall be happy. Your growing love did not escape me, and I have followed it in all its phases and seen with pleasure that it was pure, honest, and delicate."

He rang, and a servant appeared.

"Tell my daughter to come down."

A moment later Ernestine appeared, and I rose; the sight of me evidently caused her some emotion, for she blushed.

"Mademoiselle, may I interpret as favorable that flush which does not escape me? I have dared to raise my eyes to yours, to aspire to a happiness beyond my expectation, of which I shall make myself worthy; for the desire to please you makes a man capable of anything. Your parents would perhaps give me their best wishes if you were to join yours to them. Speak, and if you would know what my deportment toward you will be, should you deign to accept my homage, I shall take M. Dormeuil for a model."

Ernestine seemed to wish to speak and yet not to. I seized her hand.

"Mademoiselle, decide my fate."

"Come, daughter," said her father, "I authorize you to answer; but search your heart before doing so."

Ernestine said: "Sir, your choice does me honor, it flatters me, perhaps. Though I do full justice to your good qualities, and your delicate deportment proves that you merit such a distinction, I would like to remind you, that as yet we hardly know each other well enough to make such a momentous decision without reflection. I do indeed believe in the sincerity of your sentiments, of your love; but I cannot tell you yet that I share them. Leave me some time to myself, and since you have the permission of my parents, you can speak to me of your esteem, of . . . ," she hesitated, and I added, "of your love."

"Leave your happiness to me, for if it depends on my wishes you will soon know."

I took her hand, pressed it to my breast and to my lips. I was fairly drunk, and beside myself with joy.

"Well, well," said M. Dormeuil, "how foolish lovers are!" And turning to his wife, said "Was I so, darling?"

"Yes, my dear."

"Then I excuse him. Come, my dear Edmund, and may Ernestine soon make it possible that we may have another son."

Dormeuil came up to me. "My dear friend," he said, grasping my hand, "may you soon be my brother—that is my dearest wish."

Ernestine was standing near her father, and a sweet security seemed to spread over her whole being.

At last, I was able to say that I made daily progress in her affections, and she soon shared my love. My attentions, my courtesies, and my constancy, convinced her that she was my only love, and the reports they had of me being favorable, at the end of six months I became Ernestine's husband.

I have no words to express my happiness, and every day

71

since that memorable hour I say, "She is mine," and I reproach myself for having the slightest desire of which she is not the whole object. We were in a very heaven of bliss, and since I was staying with the Dormeuils, we were as one family. My Colonel, who had just been made a General, and who had, at the time of my marriage been particularly kind to me, added his requests to the claims which I might have to secure his regiment for me, in which I soon had young Dormeuil, much to the delight of Ernestine and our parents.

War broke out again suddenly, and I received orders to leave at once and rejoin the army assembling on the banks of the Rhine. Ernestine was unable to subdue her grief, but having in mind only my honor and reputation, she said to me: "Go, and do not fail where duty calls you. Remember that half of my life goes with you; and may fate be so kind as to give me back my husband."

It was with intense pain that I left my beloved; my parents promised to take special care of her, and ere long I found myself with the army at its mobilization center. Hostilities began immediately, and victory smiled upon us continually. My regiment performed great feats, and I had the good fortune to distinguish myself.

I had frequent letters from Ernestine, and wrote to her often. She wrote of her fears and her love, and I tried to reassure her. Dormeuil, who never left me, won distinction and promotion by his bravery.

I shall not here recite a long series of brilliant successes, nor shall I dwell upon certain fatal reverses. Having been made a General, I had under my command an army corps, and struggled against an enemy much stronger than us. Having, after a total defeat, exhibited too much attachment for

one whom I felt I owed a great deal, and fearing to be persecuted, I made up my mind to leave the country. I decided
to go to the United States.

Ernestine, still the most beautiful and loving of women,
would not desert me, and exhibited qualities which I had not
suspected she possessed.

It was with extreme grief that our parents waved us farewell. I embarked with Ernestine from Le Havre, aboard
the brig, *Swallow*, and after a rather dangerous crossing,
one which Ernestine stood better than might have been
hoped, we landed at New York where we found many
Frenchmen.

Joseph Bonaparte had been living there for some time,
quietly and unostentatiously, like a private citizen, seeming to forget with pleasure that he had held the first rank
in society, for a greensward was his throne. The only old
habit he retained was that of doing good, and never was an
unfortunate person turned away from his door. If the aid
he was able to render was less than might have been hoped
for, he nevertheless put such a grace into his good deeds
that they were the more appreciated. These thoughts necessarily lead me to relate an anecdote told to me, one that
does equal honor to all those who figured in the story I am
going to make of it.

The Sieur Carit, a Frenchman and son of the postmaster
of Tours, or at least, so he pretended, who had been guilty
in 1815 of certain utterances which were regarded as sedi-
tious, was condemned to several months imprisonment.
Unwilling to submit, he took flight. Having gone to England, he soon exhausted his resources, struggled a time
against necessity, and being unable to stand the horrors of

73

poverty, decided at last to go to the United States, enlisting as a seaman on an English ship.

When he arrived in New York in June, 1815, he did not find there the aid on which he had counted, and being again without means of livelihood and not knowing to whom he might apply for subsistence, he saw himself reduced, like Gulistan, to sleeping in the open, on the grass of the parade-ground called *The Battery*.

Carit's sadness, his dejected appearance and his poverty struck the Sieur Vauversin, attaché of the French Legation with M. Hyde-Neuville, our ambassador. Vauversin had recognized in Carit a compatriot and, accosting him one day, made himself known and asked him what had brought him to this country. Carit, without hiding anything, told him all about his experiences, closing with a picture of his present misfortunes. This greatly interested the Sieur Vauversin who, although of opposite political sympathies, saw in Carit only an unfortunate fellow whom it was his duty to aid. He offered him refreshments in terms which make proffered aid more grateful and do not wound the sensibilities. By Carit's consent he treated him to a meal whose dishes were become strange through poverty. In the course of the meal, Carit spoke warmly of Napoleon and his family. Vauversin found it in his heart to excuse this outburst whose source was in gratitude, and he advised Carit to go to Joseph Bonaparte who was then in New York. Carit promised to follow this suggestion, and they separated, agreeing to meet again. Carit, losing no time, went to Joseph Bonaparte's house and asked to speak with him. He was told that Bonaparte could not be seen, but, nothing daunted, he announced that he had just arrived from France bearing important letters

74

for his majesty. He was believed because of his truthful look, and was shown into Joseph's study.

After having apologized for the unceremonious methods employed to obtain an audience, he recited his misfortunes, drawing a most striking picture of the frightful predicament in which he found himself, having nothing and dying of hunger. Joseph answered him, "I am sorry I can do nothing for you just now. Before long I shall see: leave me your address." Carit had no residence, but gave the address of a Frenchman whom he saw every day, and went out.

He wandered sadly about the streets of New York, returning mechanically to the house of the man whose address he had given. This man was standing in the doorway, and seeing Carit from a distance, made him a sign to hasten. But Carit walked slowly, little suspecting the happy surprise Fate had prepared for him. At last he arrived, and the Frenchman said to him: "Come, my friend, rejoice; fortune smiles upon you," at the same time giving him fifty dollars, telling him that a man whom he recognized as being in Joseph Bonaparte's service, had left this sum, without either asking for a receipt or saying from whence the money came.

It is easy to imagine Carit's emotion and how grateful he was. When we learned of this, we said: "Only Frenchmen could act in this way: no matter where you may find them, in Europe or in the New World, their hearts are always open to that which is fine and great, noble and generous." I am not partisan in my thoughts, for C, J, and V are the same in my sight; the first was unfortunate and the other two did their duty.

I lived rather quietly in New York without any plan, little thinking what I should do, enjoying an easy life with Ernestine, who was my all. "One's country is where one's loved ones are," we often repeated to each other.

I met one day a French officer I had known in the army, who told me that within a few days he was leaving for Philadelphia; and when I was taken with the desire to know that city, Ernestine, who always shared my judgments, consented. We boarded a ship which was on the point of sailing and soon arrived, for the weather was as beautiful as it was favorable.

The French who were there had conceived the design of establishing a colony in Texas, on the Gulf of Mexico, near the Trinity River. Several of the Generals suggested that I go with them, and I accepted the proposal, after having first discussed the matter with Ernestine, who saw everything on the bright side so long as she was with me.

We left for New Orleans, where we laid up for some time in order to add certain necessities to our supply of provisions; and there Generals Lallemand and Rigaud, with his two children, joined us. We went down the Mississippi and, setting full sail for the Gulf of Mexico, came to Galveston Island, near the mouth of the Trinity River. This island, covered with arid sand, is inhabited by a few privateers who pray upon the Gulf, chief of whom is M. Lafitte.

There we pitched camp, until we should go to Texas. During this time hunting and fishing were our principal occupations. Deer were very numerous on the island, and one day I caught a fawn which I brought to Ernestine, who fed it with the greatest care and made it very gentle. Fish were also abundant. When the excursions were not too long, Ernestine would go with me, and we would stroll along the sea-shore. She saw a good deal of General Rigaud's daughter who, another Antigone, was ministering to the old age of her father, the later reigning supreme as General. Perfect unity existed among all the colonists.

Our party consisted of about four hundred men, several women and some children. Ernestine was beloved and revered of the whole colony and was, so to speak, its guardian angel. How proud I was to belong to you, to be your slave, your friend, your lover and your husband!

We remained about a month and a half on that island, and the stay was in no wise disagreeable. This existence, monotonous for everyone, was much less so to me; for I could see Ernestine, who inspired industry and kindness, and multiplied good deeds without end. The days flew past for her with an extraordinary swiftness.

At least, during the first days of March, 1818, General Lallemand arrived, bringing with him a number of other colonists. His arrival had been eagerly awaited, for we were anxious to proceed up the river and establish our settlement.

The camp became a busy place as we began the necessary preparations for crossing the bay and passing the Trinity, to found on Texas soil our Champ d'Asile, for that was to be the name of our colony. Each one of us in his own plans forgot the past and was absorbed in the present without anticipating the future. I had supplied myself with grain and seeds in Philadelphia and New Orleans. Ernestine would often say to me: "I shall become a farmer's wife; I shall have a flock and watch my lambs play on the pararie," and the idea of a pastoral life afforded her some happy moments. Some times she would return in memory to France, and the thought of her parents made her heart beat fast and

77

brought tears to her eyes. But she would gaze at me, her hand lying in mine, and say, "I am with you; what have I to regret? What more could I desire?"

I am scarcely the master of my thoughts, for Ernestine occupies them; everything in my eyes gives way before this overpowering emotion. I must return to our departure from Galveston.

Finally, on the 10th of March, it was decided that we should leave the island and make for the mainland. At the hour set for departure we went aboard, having fixed on the head of the bay as the meeting place.

I was with Ernestine in a little sloop I had bought in Galveston. It was almost filled by our baggage, and my wife had with her the little fawn of which I have spoken, lying at her feet. I had also four sailors to handle the boat. Generals Lallemand and Rigaud had used all possible means to preserve order in this fleet. In that particular I have only the highest praise for their foresight; just as throughout this narrative of Texas I shall have but good words for these two brave gentlemen.

We set sail, the wind sending us ploughing through the waves, led us to expect that the short crossing would be a fortunate one, for we had hardly four leagues to make. Scarcely had we issued from the bay and struck the open water, when the wind changed, became violent, and in hardly an instant scattered our boats. The night was very dark, and we had no compass, no light. How should we steer? High waves dashed over the sloop; water poured in; and we were soon drenched. My sailors were kept busy emptying the sloop; one of them held the tiller and tried to reassure us. I was concerned only for Ernestine, who showed not the slightest fear, and, if I sought to conceal the danger from her, she would smilingly say: "I am with you." What a woman! Adored one, where did you find such strength, energy, sweetness, and goodness? Ah! in your soul, happy refuge of all that is fine, great, generous and sublime!

Our position was extremely critical, for the wind blew with fury, and the roaring of the waves blended with the howls of the tempest, while at intervals we could hear our unfortunate companions firing their guns in signal of distress. At last, in spite of the difficulty, I was able to reach the appointed place, no worse off except for a wetting, and although I trembled for Ernestine's comfort, she dispelled my fears. We soon found ourselves among a large group, and fires were lighted in an effort to rally the remainder of the ships. They arrived at last, some of them having been obliged to cast overboard a portion of their cargoes, and in our position this was an irreparable loss, but several sloops had begun to leak so badly that such a sacrifice was necessary. One bark which went on a sand bar was towed off when day came, but another, not so fortunate, sank with a loss of all but one of the seven colonists who manned it, and this one, an excellent swimmer, escaped a watery grave only after infinite difficulties. As it was, he fell senseless and almost dying the moment he reached land. He was immediately cared for, and wrapped up in what we could find. Ernestine had among our baggage a woolen blanket with which we covered the unfortunate fellow. Then she sat down, and, taking his head in her lap, made him smell a bottle she had with her. It was only then that he came to himself. His first glance was for her, and, recognizing her, he smiled and said in an enfeebled voice, "Madame, what kindness," and Ernestine cried out with delight that he was saved.

We gathered around the interesting group, sharing the enthusiasm of her whom every one called the Angel of Mercy. We did not have to mourn the loss of this comrade; but those whom death had snatched from us were the focus of our attention and objects of sincere grief.

We were all together on the 11th, but on that day, and for several days following, bad weather prevented our heading for the coast. On the 14th we succeeded in reaching land and tarried there until the 16th. Then Generals Lallemand and Rigaud announced to us their intention of going on foot to the proposed site, with a detachment of a hundred men. The flotilla would go up the river under the command of an officer who was given necessary instructions. In accordance with this plan the land party took provision for two days and departed. Promising to leave no stone unturned to join them promptly, we ourselves set sail up the river.

We soon lost sight of each other, and the little fleet entered into a sort of very wide bay. We left the mainland to the right and Galveston Island to the left, heading for the mouth of the Trinity, in the most superb weather.

Gaiety soon resumed its sway; the past was only a bad dream, and we seized with avidity upon the joys of the present; everything pointed to a pleasant future. Happy songs were heard; breezes swayed our streaming banners; our sailing seemed a fête, a veritable pleasure party. Ernestine sang with the men, who were most optimistic, while I was fairly drunk with enthusiasm. I heard with delight my wife's voice, and, pressing the sorceress's pretty hand, my imagination went straying away: already I saw our dreams realized, and in fancy descried dolphins drawn to our course by the sound of her sweet singing.

Although we were moving under full sail, the second day slipped by without our having seen the mouth of the Trinity, and uncertainty, which already disturbed us, increased to such a point that we despaired for our comrades, whom we knew to be without food. Our anxiety was shared by the commander of the fleet. We steered to the right a few degrees, and finally succeeded in finding the mouth of the river. All of us were very sad, and the deepest silence lay over our ships, for we were overcome with the fear that our comrades were dying of hunger. Ernestine's state of mind was hard to describe, for she regretted not having gone with them.

"If I could share their misfortunes," she repeated, "I would be less unhappy."

Having moved against contrary currents, we did not arrive at the appointed place until six days after our departure, and it was not until then that we were able to rejoin our comrades. In what a state we found them! Pale and undone, weakened, like the shadows which we are told roam the shores of the River Styx. To escape the torments of hunger, they sought for some edible plant, and thinking they had found one, all ate of it save General Lallemand and the chief surgeon. But it was a poisonous plant, whose harmful effects they soon felt in that they fell to the ground in a most frightful state, with all the symptoms of death. Those who saw them were themselves unable to help the stricken ones, for where was a remedy to be found? Recourse to another plant might but aggravate the harm already done, for everything around seemed poisonous. Just when they were fearing that there was nothing left for their companions but the tomb, an Indian appeared in their midst. Astonished at what he saw, he asked by a sign what was the cause of the trouble. They were about to explain when he caught sight of the remains of the plant. That was enough. He departed like the wind and returned as quickly with bunches of fruit he had gathered. He pressed the juice into a vessel hanging at his belt and poured some of the liquid into the mouth of each of the sufferers who lay lifeless upon the ground. Soon they began to stir and then to rise as if from a long and painful fainting spell. At this the good savage turned in the direction of the sun, threw himself upon his knees, raised his eyes and hands towards that kind heavenly body, pronounced certain words which were unintelligible to his hearers, seeming to thank the sun for what it had done.

"Good savage, how many of the great of this earth, surrounded by pomp and riches—which they could put to such a precious use—have ever felt such a joy as must have moved your simple heart! You restored the happiness of four hundred people, for if we did not share the fate of our comrades, their death would have been, nevertheless, a calamity for us. Oh, kind Indian, gratitude raises an altar to you in our hearts, and your memory shall live on forever."

He was of the *Cochatis* nation; and his name became proverbial, so that in the future when one of us wanted the superlative figure of humanitarianism, we said: "He is a *Cochatis*." This word soon became Ernestine's surname, given her by him whom she had tended after his near-drowning. Every one followed his example. Ernestine was most interested in this savage; she wanted to see and hear him. "I must embrace him," she repeated with enthusiasm mixed

82

with tenderness. She inquired of all those who had been poisoned, how tall he was, what he looked like, the expression of his eyes; and twenty times she sketched the portrait of her dear *Cochatis*—as she called him—which she showed to every one. There was a resemblance, she was told, but the total effect was lacking. She wanted a column to be raised on the spot where the savage had stopped, with an inscription which would commemmorate this act of goodness and brotherly kindness.

It was soon necessary, however, for us to devote ourselves to more important occupations, and build our dwellings. The supplies, the munitions, and all that had comprised the cargo of the fleet was carried to the spot where we wished to establish the camp.

The engineers who were with the expedition laid out the settlement in a circular plan, indicating sites for the forts which were to insure our safety. Hatchets, saws, spades and picks found their way into every one's hands, and the surrounding forests soon rang to the blows of the ax. I hastened to construct a lean-to with branches, which Ernestine interwove with her delicate fingers, giving them the form and appearance of a leafy cradle. I covered the whole with the sail from my sloop, stretching it tightly so that the rain might not come through. Ernestine furnished the interior with moss; I spread dry leaves upon the ground and over these several bear skins bought at New Orleans. My baggage I put into one corner. Although our shelter was not a palace, my wife transformed it into the abode of happiness, and in it we were sheltered from the weather while waiting for our homes to be constructed. I built a sort of little park for Ernestine's deer, which was very much attached to her. He ate from her hand, knew her voice, and followed her about everywhere. Ernestine loved him dearly, and the colonists brought him food.

We worked away on the houses, using trees of a medium thickness which, cut in lengths of from six to seven feet, were driven into the ground close together and the spaces filled in with earth. Loop-holes were left in the walls on the far side from the camp so that each dwelling might be used as a fortress in case of attack. These houses, as well as the forts, were soon completed, everyone without exception, helping in the work.

Three forts were established: at the head of the camp: on the right, in the center, and on the left. The latter was connected by means of a covered roadway with two guard-houses not far from General Rigaud's house. General Lallemand's dwelling was in the center of the stockade, and the store a little to the right. The big fort, which was on the same side, defended the banks of the Trinity where our ships lay at anchor, and, in addition, covered the other forts. We had several pieces of cannon which were distributed among the several forts.

To the left and at the rear were forests, and in front, a plain which stretched away; and beyond were forests of tall trees whose branches were always green, as in the spring. In all, the site was very picturesque. The soil seemed fertile, plowing easily, and we believed that it would return an hundred-fold what was entrusted to its bosom. But these rich harvests, which we had a right to hope for, were destined not to fall beneath our scythes. Texas was to shine only an instant at its dawn, and to die before it had fully risen.

CHAMP D'ASILE.

Second View of Aiglevllie
Colony of Texas or Champ d'Asile

Our dwelling was soon ready to receive us, and we had a gay housewarming. We fêted the mistress of it; we drank to Texas, to the sons of glory, and to the happiness of the French.

I shall not insert here a geographical description of Texas, but shall attempt only to give an idea of what we saw when we were in camp. Trees which keep their leaves nearly all the year rose majestically toward heaven; bushes, such as the aloe, the red laurel, sunflowers and dahlias and magnolias, bloomed there in great profusion of color and perfume. Winding rivers watered and fertilized the country. Several kinds of quadrupeds live in the forests, and one never goes out hunting in vain, while the feathered folk, by the varied color of their plumage and their melodious songs, make Texas an enchanting spot. Ernestine, who loved flowers, transplanted several into a little plot adjoining our house, where they were cultivated with great care. In the center was a laurel-tree which promptly took root and became the principal ornament of the garden. The colonists were especially careful of it, for this tree is so beloved of the French that one might think it was for them alone that nature decorated the earth with it.

Several wild tribes coming to visit us were received with friendliness, and the General contracted alliances with them. Ernestine sought in vain for her kind *Cochatis*, who, unfortunately, was not a member of any of the deputations. These good Indians admired our camp, the order reigning there, and the military equipment which constituted its principal ornament. The spirit of friendship prevailing among us impressed their hearts, which were as simple and unaffected as their customs. They left us entirely satisfied, and were very happy to think that the peace of the colony would not be disturbed by our dusky neighbors.

General Lallemand busied himself with regulations which were, in a measure, to form the legal code of the colony. He appointed a council, of which General Rigaud was leader, and I a member, together with several others of the colonists. Our code did not need much discussion: it was founded on justice, friendship and altruism, its fundamental provisions being that all owed each other aid and protection. Property was held in common, and the common end of all endeavor was the prosperity of the colony and the happiness of the group, which in turn would rebound to the advantage of the individual. Wisdom and prudence were distinguishing characteristics of our two chiefs; and, although I had scarcely known Generals Lallemand and Riguad, I had heard them spoken of in the highest manner and now saw with pleasure that they deserved such praise.

General Rigaud, the Nestor of the colony—equally distinguished by his good qualities—inspired the liveliest interest. Surrounded by his son and daughter, who were both models of filial devotion, one might have mistaken him for Belisarius, though he still had his sight. The respect and friendship accorded him, together with his children, satisfied him entirely. Ernestine called him father, and this name, from her lips always made the old man smile and his heart throb. He was ever ready to expand to generous sentiments.

Our existence in the colony was not without its pleasures; our wants were simple, and we had what we needed; the bright future before us made us forget the occasional privations, and because everyone shared these privations alike, they were scarely noticed. Ernestine, who had known ease and luxury, was the first to adapt herself to the changed conditions. Her dwelling was for her a palace, and she was always gay and even-tempered. The serenity of her spirit—the reflection of the beautiful sky smiling down upon us—was contagious. The leaders held her up as an example, which the colonists readily accepted.

"My dear," she often said to me, "I believe that the founding of our colony will be an epochal event in history, for it will prosper, I hope, and our names will be joined in glory with the benefactors of mankind. I cannot help but feel a little pride; and if from pole to pole the Frenchman is spoken of with praise, the same must be said of the French women who are none the less praiseworthy."

These words pronounced with a certain solemnity, and rendered yet more meaningful by modesty, made me fall at her feet.

"What are you, anyhow," I would say to her, "oh, adored woman? From what divine essence are you formed?"

"Rise," she said. "You judge me with a lover's vision; I am simply a woman, endowed with certain qualities, who seeks to grow better. If I were to believe you, I would end by growing conceited, and that would destroy my own work."

I looked at her with new-found delights, repeating to myself: "To think that this treasure is mine!"

Supreme calm reigned in the colony. Plans were made for the plowing and planting of every portion of the land which belonged to us, according to the nature of the soil. Hope of a bountiful harvest inspired us, and already we could see the colony growing rich from its products. Vain hope! A clear dawn is too often the fore-runner of a storm, as we were destined to realize.

Our presence in Texas was displeasing to the Spaniards occupying the forts of San Antiono and La Bahia. They sought to incite enmity against us among the Indian tribes native to the country adjacent to Champ d'Asile, and they succeeded. And as soon as they saw they had aroused the Indians, they began to make us out usurpers who, after having disturbed the peace of Europe for more than twenty years, had come to do the same thing in the New World. It was, therefore, for the general good to drive us out before we became dangerously strong. It was decided to arm and march against us with the intent of forcing us to abandon our colony.

We learned of these hostile intentions and made ready to oppose force to force. The alarm was to be given, every one was to be ready, and the enemy was soon to know that our arms were still to be dreaded.

Ernestine saw all these preparations fearlessly, without being able, however, to keep down misgivings.

"I will follow you," she said. "If I have to die, I shall at least be at your side, or I can ward off the blows meant for you. You will see how worthy Ernestine is to be the wife of a French soldier, and although I shall not court danger, I shall see it without paling and will walk in the path of the brave."

Our first impulse had urged us to fight, but maturer consideration made us realize the danger of such a course, for although victory—which we did not doubt—might crown our banners, we knew that our enemies would arise from their own ashes; while we, abandoned by our fellow-coun-

88

trymen, decimated by starvation and famine, would soon be forced to yield.

It was decided, consequently, that we should leave the colony and retire to Galveston Island, where the sea would give us at once protection and communication with the mainland, or furnish us a passage for going elsewhere, if that seemed advisable. As soon as this decision was reached, preparations were begun for our departure. A visit to the ships showed them to be in good condition. We were not long in transporting our baggage, our supplies, our munitions, provisions, and artillery to the banks of the Trinity.

Ernestine sadly said farewell to our humble dwelling.

"Still another dream shattered," she murmured.

She watered her flowers and her laurel-tree, a branch of which she cut, called her little deer to follow her, and, turning towards Champ d'Asile, she spoke these words: "Adieu, land of exile, where we thought to find peace and perhaps happiness; we fly from thee to better climes," and, then turning towards me, "I am sorry, my dear, if, for an instant I forgot that I was with you, and that I have nothing to regret."

We walked in the direction of the river, I giving her my arm, holding my gun with the other, and soon we were at the shore where the colonists were loading the boats.

There all was activity: bales, cannon, stacked arms, farming implements; and, farther on, a fire over which was being prepared the last meal we were to take in this inhospitable land. But before our departure we were destined to witness an affecting scene.

Two of our colonists, having seen on the opposite bank some deer passing quietly by, thought they could easily approach and bag them. Without telling anyone of their plans, they got into a small canoe tied up at the bank, and crossed over, armed with their guns. We did not notice them, until they were in the middle of the stream. We paid little attention to their action, but a glance at the opposite shore explained it. They got out of their canoe, the deer fled, the two men pursued, and we lost sight of them. A few moments later we heard two shots, and one of us said, "Fanfare, hallo, the chase is over."

We heard nothing more, and it was a long time before we again gave thoughts to the hunters.

Finally meal-time arrived, and our men had not yet returned. We began to be alarmed. Ernestine herself seemed tormented by a sort of sinister foreboding.

"My dear," she said to me in fearsome accents, "could something have happened to our friends?" for she included all the colonists in this category.

I replied that I thought not, but at this moment, putting her glass to her eye, she examined the other shore and cried out, "Great heavens! There are Indians running about in the woods."

I hurriedly arose and, approaching my comrades, told them what Ernestine had seen, adding, "Let us not lose a moment in going to their assistance."

Scarcely had I uttered these words when General Lallemand cried, "To arms!" and in an instant 200 armed men surrounded him. He ordered 50 men to get into two barks and row across at once to bring back or aid the unfortunate colonists. An officer put himself at their head and the order was carried out. We soon lost sight of them in the forest, but within a short time the discharge of several guns struck our ears. We could see Indians running away, our friends in pursuit and firing at them. We knew not what to think, but all of us were a prey to fears. Ernestine was pale and trembling. After that we heard nothing more. We were considering sending out another detachment, when our comrades were seen emerging from the woods on the opposite shore, in silence and consternation. They laid something in one of the canoes, two rowers got in, and the remainder embarked in the other, towing the bark in which the two hunters had crossed the river.

We waited with impatience, anxiety even, until they should come up. When they reached the shore, they were so pale I suspected some misfortune, and I prevented Ernestine from approaching. I walked to the boats and was seized with horror to see the mangled and half-devoured bodies of our two unfortunate comrades. They had been surprised by the savages, but had defended themselves courageously, for six Indians were found in the dust, though they had at last been overpowered.

Here is the report the officer made to General Lallemand:

"Scarcely had we advanced a hundred paces into the forest when we caught sight of about sixty savages sitting in a circle, appearing very pre-occupied. Seeing on the ground the arms and the shredded clothes of our comrades, we suspected what had happened. The officer gave the command to fire, which command was so well executed that about twenty were left lying, the remainder taking flight, most of them wounded, hotly pursued by our men. One of the colonists succeeded in overtaking and dispatching two with his bayonet.

They then approached the spot of this horrible feast and found the bodies and still quivering limbs of the two unfortunate men. Ernestine, whom I rejoined, burst into tears, and we all shared her emotion. The bodies were covered, and an order immediately given to dig a grave beneath a cypress where they were to be laid. They were put into a casket which was closed with care, and when the grave was done, all the colonists, armed and marching by twos, moved away in a sad cortege. The most profound silence reigning over everything.

When we reached the grave-side the bodies were placed in it, and before the dirt was filled in I advanced and said in tones of deep feeling! "Adieu, dear friends, more fortunate than we, you have nothing more to dread from the fate which pursues us. From the other world, where doubtless you are, hear our regrets: they are sincere. May your spirits be satisfied. Farewell! You shall live forever in our hearts."

As the coffin disappeared, a general salute was fired: and there was nailed to the cypress a leaden plate on which was engraved: "Here lie two Frenchmen." Ernestine put into the newly turned earth the branch of laurel she had brought, little dreaming how it would be used, which was a fitting funeral tribute for the brave.

We left the spot, our eyes damp with tears, the new sadness which had taken possession of our souls, showing on every visage. Preparations for our departure were hastened, for this land held nothing more for us, and we had just experienced a cruel loss.

Ernestine, her eyes red, looked silently at me, weeping from time to time. "Oh, my dear," she said, "does this unfortunate beginning foretell direr misfortunes? If I were to lose you, if death, wielding his cruel scythe over the colony were to strike you, what would become of me? Ah, I would rather die a thousand times that one grave should enfold us, as our love has done in life."

Everything which remained to be loaded having been put aboard, we set sail, the wind and current favoring us. Since we had already come this way, there was no danger of mistaking the route, and soon we arrived in Galveston Bay, where we cast anchor, and promptly landed.

A new camp was laid out—for the other no longer existed. We threw up but one defence, and that for the artillery. We could not stay long on this island; we intended to delay only long enough to decide on our movements for our situation was both uncertain and precarious. Besides, since our provisions were running low, we had to see about procuring more, and these could be got only in New Orleans. It is true that we had made a contract with a merchant there, but would he fulfill it?

For diversion, fishing and hunting occupied us. There were deer on land and cormorants in the air, which fell beneath our deadly lead, and the waters of the bay furnished fish and oysters in abundance. Ernestine, the good and courageous, sometimes went with me, shod in boots, a plain straw hat on her head, wearing a simple, close-fitting dress, scarcely pressing the sand of the earth with her light step. We would return tired out in the evening, and the young deer, which she left in care of a colonist, would express his joy at seeing her by bounding about and caressing her.

But hunting and fishing could not long satisfy our needs, and supplies beginning to run low, rations were cut down; still the merchant did not appear. A month passed thus, with all of us in the same predicament. General Lallemand, distressed to see us in such a critical position, decided to go

93

to New Orleans to secure aid for us, and left, promising to let us hear from him soon.

I, too, could easily have left the colonists and Galveston Island, for I had a boat of my own, but when I mentioned my plan to Ernestine, she said: "What will become of all these poor people? For yesterday several of them said to me: 'You will stay with us? You won't abandon us? Poverty is nothing for us since you share it. You give us strength and courage. Can we complain while we see you suffer with so much resignation, you who were not made for such a fate?' Let's stay on, my dear!"

"Your wish is my law. Let us stay," I said.

General Rigaud, who assumed command of the colonists after General Lallemand's departure, spent a part of each day with Ernestine. This worthy old gentleman loved her like a daughter, and Mademoiselle Rigaud cherished her as a sister. The three of them often went walking together, reminding one of a great elm spreading its protecting branches over two young plants exposed to the north winds.

Although the colonists had the greatest confidence in General Rigaud, and although I did not try to put myself forward in the least, they often sought my advice, and I tried to harmonize everything and to encourage them in a patience and hope I did not myself share.

Famine made itself felt more and more, and distress became the keener with the appearance on the Island of an envoy from the Spanish who, having occupied Champ d'Asile after our departure, demanded that we leave Galveston also. A formal refusal was our answer, reinforced by more vigorous measures. The deputy departed, and we thought no more of the matter. If the Spanish had appeared we would have repelled their unjust aggression, but in our present situation it was wiser to gain time—prudence and dire necessity forcing us to this course.

Starvation approached with all its horrors, finding us with no means of combatting it. We still had provisions, but so few that each waning day made us fear the dawn of the morrow. If we experienced the acutest suffering, if our hearts were moved by the most persistent presentiments of evil, the atmosphere which surrounded us presented a striking contrast, for the sky was clear and cloudless, and the radiant sun rose from the waves to sink into them again at evening without even the thinnest vapor to hide it from our gaze. Kind, heavenly body, you should shine only on the happy!

We were nearing the close of a most beautiful day, and, scattered about in our camps, we were preparing to go to our several abodes, while hope which sustains a man even to the grave, seemed still to smile upon us. Ernestine leaned upon me, her little deer was following her, taking from her hands at intervals the blades of grass she held out to him. A slight breeze sprang up, and immediately, on examining the horizon, I saw a dark spot forming, which I called to the attention of everybody. All agreed that it portended a change in the weather. This consciousness aroused no uneasiness, however.

Night fell; Morpheus distributed his gifts, and sweet dreams brought forgetfulness of our ills and cradled us in the chimeras of foolish and vain hopes.

Suddenly a terrible detonation shook us from our sleep. The unleashed tempest, the wild waves beat upon the land, while the rain fell in torrents. The sky was ablaze, and the stakes that held our cabin gave away and broke. The canvas which covered it tore away, and I caught sight of a water-spout bringing death and destruction in its wake. The sea was rushing in from all sides. Ernestine, standing, held on with her delicate arms to one of the supports of our dwelling, and I supported her with difficulty against the tide, which beset us from all directions. A gust of wind tore away the last shred of cloth which sheltered us. A flash of lightning showed me Ernestine's features bespeaking the serenity of resignation.

"Hold me in your arms," she said, "and may the tomb unite in death those whom the sweetest love has joined in life."

I was just going to answer, when, from the depths of the waves that rushed about us, there came a cry, "Help! Help!" Ernestine, tearing herself from me, deaf to all save the voice of duty, darted away and seized the arm of the unhappy man who called out. I, who had not had time to prevent her, saw her disappear in the surroundings. But fortunately, by the aid of lightning flashes, I was able to find her and raise her up, together with him who owed his life to her, and who now was strong enough to help me hold her above the water. This frightful struggle lasted through the night, till dawn paling the horizon gave promise of coming day. In lulls of the wind, cries and wails could be heard on every hand, to be immediately drowned by the wind's redoubled fury.

Day came at last to shed its light upon a scene of desolation like the great flood, which one of our best painters has so well portrayed, showing in actuality that which art can but feebly imitate. The tempest was not yet subsiding, but now that we could see the danger, it was easier to avoid.

We could carry aid to the stricken and save them from death. Ernestine seemed to be endowed with supernatural strength and did not leave my side. Our friends cried to her to spare herself, but she replied that she wished to save them, and assisted in carrying the wounded into the strongest building, around which we all gathered.

Galveston Island seemed a part of the sea that inundated it, and this scene of destruction became more terrible when the wind and waves, renewing their fury, broke the chains holding our boats and carried them out to sea, thus destroying our means of escape. I dared not impart such news, the words died on my lips. Ernestine, who saw me shiver, asked, "What is the matter?"

"It is nothing," I answered, and my words seemed to give her a hope which had forever abandoned me. The sea, seeming at last satisfied with its crowning blow, began to grow calm, and the waters to subside into the gulf.

Since we were on a kind of elevation, that portion was soon drained, and we could sit down. But what sights met our eyes! We were all livid and discolored; our soaked clothes clung so closely to our bodies that they seemed to be a part of our skin. We were, furthermore, devoured by a burning thirst, and sea water was all nature offered us.

We noticed several barrels floating in a kind of lake the waves had formed, and when some of the men pushed them ashore, they were found to contain water. O Providence! You had not yet abandoned us, for that water saved our lives!

I was concerned only for Ernestine, who, for her part, forgetting what she had gone through, was caring for everyone and carrying water to those too weak to get it for themselves. Mademoiselle Rigaud was with her father, who had thoughts only for her.

At last there was quiet, and if nature's calm had not as yet entered our souls, our dangers were less frightful.

Several ships were discovered on the bay-side by some of the colonists who had gone hunting, and we could thus communicate with the mainland.

I learned that several of the island's natives possessed provisions they were carefully hiding, but when I went to them and offered gold, they replied they had nothing to spare. When I returned empty-handed, Ernestine said, "I'll go," and taking more gold and diamonds, she departed, accompanied by Mademoiselle Rigaud.

About an hour afterwards, I saw her coming back with about twenty men who were bringing to our camp what they had refused me, for they had been unable to resist the argument of the gold and jewels, combined with Ernestine's sweet, persuasive eloquence. She returned to camp, happiness lighting up her face. It was like the Graces leading in *Plenty*, and everyone's blessings accompanied these two revered beings.

General Rigaud thanked Ernestine for having included his daughter in this good deed, and pressed her to his heart. I was more delighted than the others, for I said to myself, "That consoling angel is mine, Divine Creature! My one heart does not suffice to adore you as you merit! It is too little for my voice to say each instant, 'I love you.' "

These provisions were sufficient only for the moment, and a clear view of our situation showed us a future more terrible still, for want would soon make itself felt again; and there was still no news of General Lallemand, although more than a month had elapsed since his departure. As fishing and hunting could not supply our needs, it was decided to send the General's son to New Orleans. When he left a ray of hope shone in our eyes, only to die after a considerable time was elapsed.

We seemed to be in an unknown and forgotten world, without news of any kind, where despair would soon take possession of every man's soul. It was decided that we should leave this cursed land which begrudged us an existence, and seemed wearied of our presence in it.

I sacrificed my remaining gold to purchase for our brothers what the inhabitants of the island would consent to sell.

There were some who chose to go overland to other places, having no fixed destination, and these were taken to the mainland. Others decided to embark in the remaining ships and set sail for the United States.

The provisions and supplies were divided among the colonists, and I placed in my sloop as much as I could secure without depriving the others. I took with me, to man the little ship, six of the men who had served in the navy.

We said good-bye to each other, and, after having called on Fortune to aid us, we separated. I went aboard where Ernestine already was with her little deer, while our friends from the shore wished us a fortunate journey. Ernestine had been very dear to them, and tears stained all cheeks. Ernestine stretched out her arms toward the shore and a last good-bye was heard.

The sail spread, the wind filled it, we went plowing along through the waves of the Gulf of Mexico until we lost sight of Galveston Island and our friends whom we could see for a long time on the seashore. The wind continuing favorable, we sailed along the coast, came to La Belise at the mouth of the Mississippi, and went up this river as far as New Orleans. A few days later the remainder of the colonists who left by boat arrived, and then others who came overland, having experienced terrible hardships.

The citizens of New Orleans welcomed us with the kindness which is misfortune's due, and soon the dire traces of want and privation could no longer be seen. Ernestine had suffered greatly from the continual agitation in which we lived at Galveston. A few days' rest and quiet should have restored her, but she grew extremely weak and fell into a despondency which was all the more dangerous because she tried to conquer it in order not to frighten me. I consulted a physician who advised the most careful attention, if her health was not to be compromised. What a frightful effect these words had on me!

"Do not worry"; he said, "the remedy is at hand, and in a few days your wife will be restored to you in all her grace and freshness."

He kept his word, and this man was for me the god of Epidaurus.

I learned through one of the colonists that a certain merchant of the city was seeking me, I hastened to him and identified myself. He gave me letters from our parents, telling us that the bearer was to pay us two hundred thousand francs, and that we would soon see them, together with the remainder of their fortune, which they had turned into money in order to be able—together with my brother—to come and join us. They were to embark at Ostende on the ship *The Two Friends*, which was leaving for New Orleans.

I flew with this good news to Ernestine, who, as soon as

she saw the letter in my hand, said it was from her mother, while tears flowed from her eyes as she pressed the dear writing to her lips and heart. After having read the letters, she cried: "My happiness is going to be still greater, and I shall have nothing left to wish for."

The doctor was there.

"That is worth more than all my remedies," he said joyfully, and a few days later she was much better and soon completely recovered.

I bought a charming house on the river bank, and we went to housekeeping when I had made certain improvements and changes necessary for the proper reception of our parents. Soon everything was as we wished. Ernestine, having arranged the garden like the one she had in France where we had first seen each other in the early days of our affection, repeated to me constantly that her love for me grew from day to day. We were in perfect accord, and were husband and wife without ever having ceased to be lovers.

Two months passed, when, one morning, hearing two shots from a cannon, I inquired and was informed that a vessel entering the harbor was saluting the city.

"Oh, Papa and Mama and my brother are arriving!" Ernestine exclaimed. And we, together with our merchant friend, went down to the docks.

The ship was casting anchor, and all the passengers and crew were on the bridge. We looked closely and soon saw our dear parents, who recognized us, too. Ernestine uttered a cry of joy. The small boat was launched, we approached, and a moment later we pressed to our hearts the best of fathers, the tenderest of mothers, and my brother.

We soon told them the story of our misfortunes, which excited and astonished them and made them tremble for our lives. What Ernestine had done seemed incomprehensible to them, and they could not realize it.

Our parents, who were possessed of a considerable fortune, purchased several pieces of property, having resolved no more to leave the country which had given them back their children; and my brother swore to remain with us always. Ernestine poured out her good deeds for the benefit of those colonists who might be in need of help, and did it with so much delicacy and so much consideration for the pride of each that her efforts were the more appreciated.

We are now established in New Orleans, far from the storms and revolutions which are the curse of nations and the affliction of men. We still love our mother-country, and her welfare is our dearest wish; but we have no regrets, for destiny, which separated us for a moment, as if to try us, has united us again. Peace and happiness are our lot. If we have anything more to thank Providence for, it is that she has from time to time given us the opportunity of making others happy.

Ernestine, the best of daughters and of wives, who soon will be the tenderest of mothers, is still what she was when I first set eyes upon her dear face, the model of all that is most perfect in Nature's work.

As for me, after having pursued with some distinction that most honorable of all careers, after having obtained those rewards which alone are prized by soldiers, and which embellish his laurels, I am giving up everything, and returning to the obscurity of civil life, intending no longer to concern myself with any one but those who make life precious to me, and whose happiness it is my pleasure and duty to insure.

I have witnessed a great many events which have influenced profoundly the destiny of states, and I have known men who have played more or less interesting rôles; I have seen schemes vanish into thin air, reputations lost, ambitions which were theirs by right given up to nothingness; I have understood the schemes by which many people expected to gain their ends—the first have inspired me with pity and the second with scorn. As for me, always faithful to my duties, and never having swerved from the path of honor, I can say, now that I have retired into solitude—

"*Felix qui potui rerum cognoscere causas.*"

We cannot bring our story to a close without giving our readers *The Song of Texas*. These couplets were written by Edmund, and Ernestine composed the music for them. She would sing them to the colonists with such touching expression, such true interpretation, as to electrify them all, and they would then repeat in chorus with the greatest enthusiam, the last two lines of each stanza.

THE SONG OF TEXAS

Frenchmen, if a fate unruly
Drove us from our native land,
We shall still revere her truly,
Though forgot on every hand.
Only Honor lies behind us,
Peace within our hearts we feel;
Happiness has come to find us.—
The laurel grows in Champ d' Asile.

Recollections here surround us,
We shall never more complain ;
Warrior's joys that here are round us
Sweeter are than fortune's gain.
We shall sing of our past glories
At the oxen's earth-clogged heel ;
Music to us are those stories—
The laurel grows in Champ d' Asile.

Glory has her names to cherish,
Echoing on every hand ;
Soldiers, lest their fame should perish,
Let them ring through Texas Land.
For our God-like ones we're praying,
Servile words our lips would seal ;
In other lands they will be saying—
The laurel grows in Champ d' Asile.

TEXAS

OR

AN HISTORICAL STUDY

OF

CHAMP D'ASILE

*Comprising all that has happened from the forma-
tion to the dissolution of that Colony, with the
causes, and a list of all the French Colonists, together with useful information for their families,
and a map of the camp.*

DEDICATED TO

The Gentlemen Who Subscribed to the Enterprise in Favor of the Refugees;

By

Messrs. Hartmann and Millard, members of
the Champ d'Asile Colony, recently
returned to France

LE TEXAS,

OU

NOTICE HISTORIQUE

SUR

LE CHAMP D'ASILE,

Comprenant tout ce qui s'est passé depuis la formation jusqu'à la dissolution de cette Colonie, les causes qui l'ont amenée, et la liste de tous les Colons français, avec des renseignemens utiles à leurs familles,

et le plan du camp,

DÉDIÉ A MESSIEURS LES SOUSCRIPTEURS
en faveur des Réfugiés ;

Par MM. HARTMANN ET MILLARD, *Membres du Champ d'Asile, nouvellement de retour en France*

A PARIS,

Chez BÉGUIN, éditeur, rue Jean-Pain-Mollet, n° 10 ;
BÉCHET aîné, libraire *de la Renommée*, quai des Augustins, n. 57 ;
DELAUNAY, libraire, Galerie de Bois, Palais-Royal.
ET A GAND, *chez* HOUDIN, Imprimeur-Libraire, de l'Université.

JUIN 1819.

Facsimile of the Title Page of the Original Edition of *Le Texas*

Dedication

*TO THE GENTLEMEN WHO SUBSCRIBED TO THE
ENTERPRISE IN FAVOR OF THE REFUGEES*

Gentlemen:
*To dedicate to you an exact account of what transpired in our un-
dertaking, which you desired to see prosper, is to perform a sacred
duty. We, more fortunate than many of our comrades, have seen
again that dear fatherland which we so regretfully left, of which
we held such sweet remembrances. Thus it is our privilege to convey
to you the sentiments expressed on the banks of the Trinity by Frenchmen always worthy of the name, when they learned that their brothers
on the Seine desired not only to lighten the sorrow of absence, but
to share with them in the land of their exile such happiness as they
could enjoy far from the generous hands to which they were beholden
for this good fortune.*

*Proud of having aroused the lively interest of the most distin-
guished citizens of the greatest nation of the universe, the Texas Colonists hoped to show themselves worthy of it by determined efforts to
attain prosperity which would justify the good wishes and help of
their compatriots. With what pride could they, these sons of France
—so far from her—see the products of Champ d'Asile borne to the
feet of their mother, as the first fruits of its gifts, as a tribute of
their unwavering love for her.*

Alas! Your noble designs were not fulfilled, and our sweet dreams have been dispelled. Deprived of the aid which you intended for us, we saw d'Asile destroyed—the refuge which you had been pleased to imagine would see the peaceful end of our days which has been but too long and stormy. Envy, having fallen asleep in the old world, reawakened in the new to punish us for the glory of our country to which, we dare say, some of us had contributed. Scattered over several parts of the Americas, the greater number of our companions have no hope but in your generosity ; it is by means of funds collected in this munificent spirit—to assure us a new country—that they can return to their homes. More unfortunate than they were when your generosity attempted to better their lot, they would not hesitate to leave behind them the horror of their present destiny ; and in the march of human events, your kindness will be attended by their gratitude.

Believing, Gentlemen, that you are always anxious to protect Frenchmen, so often victims of circumstances which they could neither forsee nor avoid, we make so bold, then, as to publish, under your good auspices, a work destined to make known their past misfortunes, and to arouse again in their behalf the sympathy of which they are more than ever in need, we have the honor to be with respect,

> *Gentlemen,*
> *Your very humble and very obedient servants*

Preface

The events which preceded and followed the 20th of March, 1815, engendered in France a sort of fermentation, which embittered every spirit. Everywhere hopes had been dashed to earth. Those who had seen them come to life no longer troubled to hide their hatred. Words of proscription, of vengeance were heard; and, although the government's head did not speak out in terms which certain individuals might have desired, the order of the 24th of July, in forcing a number of Frenchmen to expatriate themselves, aroused in others the desire to go to another hemisphere.

America was the place which the greater number chose, and soon Champ d'Asile appeared as a refuge to those who were afraid of coming under the ban of that law of the 24th of July, and to others, who, seeing themselves obliged to give up a calling which they had followed with honor for many years, thought they could not do better than to try their fortunes in another land, having as their only capital the most glorious of memories, that fortitude which knows how to face adversity, and the courage which aids in surmounting difficulties that industry may triumph Such were the causes which brought about this emigration, which wrung tears from the eyes of love and friendship, and which concentrated the gaze of a great part of the French upon this spot on the new continent, where brothers, companions in arms, were going to found another fatherland.

Time, which stills everything and shapes the future, let it be supposed that the light of forgiveness might yet shine, that the past would be lost in forgetfulness, and that a propitious future might bring back to the bosoms of their families men who were guilty only of mistakes passion had distorted into crime. It was not thought that hatred had struck such deep roots into our souls, that, at the moment when the enlightened representatives of a noble and generous people should ask the government to open its heart to benevolence by recalling the exiles, the terrible and fearful word *never* would be heard, like the voice of destiny pronouncing its unchanging decree.

Is then the heart of him who pronounced it thrice brassbound? Can it be more inexorable than Providence? I ask this of those who each instant invoke the Eternal, who paint religion to us as the only good which can be sought on earth while giving us the hope of a better world. Was it religion that inspired him who caused that "never" to resound within those walls where our legislators discuss laws which ought to insure our happiness? NO! You altar-ministers, you who bring consolation to the man who is going down into the tomb, you who calm the remorse of the criminal about to expiate his sins through deserved punishment, you let a ray of hope shine into his heart, and "never" does not escape your lips: you are for him the forerunners of mercy, and, thanks to you, he is launched into eternity without fear. Are they then more guilty, that they are cast aside with such a coldly deliberate hatred? And if the most sacred dogmas proclaim that there is no pardon for which one may not hope, why should we show ourselves more unrelenting than Him from whom everything emanates? Oh, you who are called on to pronounce upon the fate of your fellows, learn that he is cruel who is only just.

We are far from thinking that the King, in whose name the word was spoken, sanctioned this term of reprobation. No! The heart of a father is a spring of the sweetest, the tenderest affection, and this thought is for us a healing balm.*

We do not claim the power of pre-vision; our wishes cannot be considered as derogatory to authority; one then cannot blame them. Besides, who, during the past twenty years, has nothing to reproach himself for? Who has not made a few mistakes? Must we always be divided? Let us everywhere forget that we have followed different ways; let us reunite as if we had just taken a long and painful journey, and forget in the bosom of friendship and sweet confidence the fatigues and hardships of the trial.

Who can hold vain self-love and foolish pride? What sacrifice should one not make for one's country? You would give your life for her. What you are refusing her is a far lesser thing.

It is time that all Frenchmen were united, that they comprised one family. Let us return to our early character, let us add color of reason to our natural gaiety, which will bring out the first without harming the second. After having been too shallow, let us not try to be too deep; and in avoiding an eccentricity let us not commit a fault and even a vice.

We are going to try to sketch the picture of what happened

* We were not mistaken in this. His majesty has allowed Marshall Soult, Messrs. Dirat Pommereuil, and several others, to return to France.

to certain Frenchmen in a place where hope led them and fatality has pursued them. Was it to teach them that they were not born to those climes and that their country called them back? Time, we like to believe, will prove to us whether we have seen into the future.

We advise our readers that our narrative bears the stamp of exact truth. We do not aspire to the rank of authors; we, the simple actors in all that has happened, shall be the true historians of it. Faults will be found in the style of this work, inaccuracies which a more facile pen would have avoided. We beg, then, the indulgence of our readers. Soldiers know their swords and the art of war better than they do the flowers of rhetoric.

A work on Champ d'Asile has already appeared which contains rather extensive details about that country. What we are offering to the public is a simple recital of the events which have transpired during our sojourn in Texas, between our departure and our return passage to France. This is, strictly speaking, only a journal, which will, we hope, be of interest to those who sometimes thought of us when we were beyond the seas.

ACCOUNT OF WHAT HAPPENED IN TEXAS FROM THE TIME OF THE ESTABLISHMENT OF THE FRENCH REFUGEES IN THAT PROVINCE UNTIL THEIR DEPARTURE

Chapter First

MR. HARTMANN'S JOURNAL

LEAVING STRASBOURG FOR AMSTERDAM

EMBARKATION & CROSSING

ARRIVAL AT NEW YORK

AFTER HAVING FOLLOWED A military career as much from preference as from the force of events which obliged the French to take up arms in defense of their country; having returned to civil life with no intention of again joining the army; and being still of an age when idleness is a crime and a theft from the society to which we are responsible; I formed the project of going to the United States. In those distant climes I expected to meet success, or at least a moderate fortune. This resolution taken, I busied myself with putting it into effect. Having assembled my resources, I left my family and Strasbourg, my birthplace, in the month of May, 1817, to go to Amsterdam, which I had chosen as my port of embarkation.

Arrived in that city, I stayed there until the month of July, and after having made all the necessary arrangements, on the 3rd of July I boarded the American ship, *Brick-Ohio*, captain, E. Carmann, which was sailing for New York.

The 3rd of July we heaved anchor and put to sea at 4 o'clock in the morning with west winds blowing. At 9 o'clock we passed the Pampus, at 1 o'clock we were running between Usek and Eukeisen, and we dropped anchor there in the evening on account of the calm.

On the 4th we set sail at 4 o'clock in the morning under an east wind. On that day the crew celebrated the anniversary of the Independence of the United States, and at 11 o'clock we anchored in the roadstead of the Textel.

From the 5th to the 9th of July the winds from the west were very violent. We rode at anchor in order to take on the water and other provisions necessary for the voyage which we were going to undertake. On the 10th of July we were under sail at 4 o'clock in the morning, but the calm forced us to cast anchor; at 11 o'clock we raised it, set sail with the east wind, and in the afternoon we lost sight of land, the wind blowing S. S. E.

On the 11th of July the wind veered to the west and the weather was very foggy. We changed course in the afternoon and headed north in order to round Scotland. In the evening the weather was fine with a great number of ships in sight. On the 12th we resumed our course with the east winds. The weather was rainy. At 10 o'clock a pilot-ship from Yarmouth hailed us and at 11 another. In the evening we had fine weather.

On the 13th we tacked about in front of the canal, with the wind southwest; at 7 o'clock rain. At 8 o'clock the wind moved to the northwest, blowing briskly, at 11 o'clock we could see the beacons on the coast of England.

The 14th, the weather and the wind did not change and we saw again the beacon; the lead was cast, found bottom at 21 fathoms. On the 15th, wind southwest; the morning, rain; the afternoon, calm.

On the 16th, at 4 o'clock in the morning, we entered the canal with an east wind; at 8 o'clock we saw the coasts of France and of England; at 10 o'clock the wind shifted to the northeast; it was blowing briskly, and we put her head-on; at noon the wind lessened somewhat and several sails were hauled up.

The 17th, same wind, clear weather. During the after-noon the wind shifted to the southwest and we passed Bracheead.

The 18th we were in sight of the Isle of Wight, north wind.

From the 19th to the 31st of July continuing contrary winds, and we tacked about in front of the Lizar Cape.

First to the 2d of August, fine weather, wind northwest; in the afternoon, wind blowing briskly, a heavy sea, and we were obliged to put her headon.

The 3d and the 4th, same weather; in the afternoon it cleared and we had calm.

The 5th and 6th, fine weather, east wind, but calm; the afternoon two young sharks were taken, about 6 feet long.

From the 7th to the 15th, still a contrary wind and bad weather, the sea very rough. Afternoon we spoke to the English brig, *The Sophia*, of Bristol, from Milford Haven, bound for Newfoundland, at sea twenty days, and it gave us the longitude; at five o'clock another ship in sight.

From the 16th to the 19th same weather and same wind.

20th. North wind and calm.

21st. Calm. In the evening we had a slight breeze from the S.W.

22d. Wind northwest; in the evening the wind settled into the north blowing very briskly.

23rd. Wind E. S. E., calm; the evening a breeze from the W.

24th. Southwest wind, continual rain.

From the 25th to the 28th, same weather, very warm; in the evening the wind shifted to the north.

29th to the 30th. Wind N. N. E. At daybreak we saw away to the W.S.W. Graciosa, one of the Azores islands, fine weather. At ten o'clock, the sight of St. George and Tercere, and a three-masted Dutch boat heading east; at noon we saw the famous mountain-peak, and at three o'clock the island of Fayal.

31st. Wind N.N.E. In sight of the above islands, and we headed for Fayal. At six o'clock we saw a three-master which steered for us. At seven o'clock her ship's boat came alongside, and we learned that it was a Dutch boat, named *The America*, coming from Batavia and bound for Amsterdam, having eleven days of sailing ahead of her.

We bought of her two bales of rice, and we wished each other bon voyage. Towards evening, almost calm, we sailed between Picko and Fayal, west wind; at 8 o'clock we anchored in the roadstead of Fayal, in 20 fathoms of water; at midnight a great west wind rose and we were obliged to throw out our main anchor.

In the evening, before anchoring, our captain went aboard a three-masted Dutchman who was in the roadstead in order to secure information about landing; he was informed of the location of the currents which would undoubtedly have cast us upon the rocks. We put our skiff into the water with the purpose of towing the ship into port.

On the first of September, in the morning, we signaled to have the customs men sent on board; they arrived shortly after the declaration had been made; the captain, as well as the passengers, who numbered ten, went ashore in order to purchase enough necessaries for the remainder of the voyage. There were several English and Dutch ships in the harbor.

I cannot give many details about this island for we stayed there only a day: it has considerable trade in Picko wines, which are excellent; the harbor is small, but fine and safe.

The 2d of September. Wind N.N.E. fresh; at 8 o'clock the customs officers returned aboard, and shortly afterwards we heaved anchor and set sail; in the afternoon we lost sight of land; the 3d, calm; the 4th, south wind; the 5th, calm; the 6th, N.E. wind; in the morning we spoke to a Spanish schooner, coming from Porto Rico and bound for Santa Maria, having fifteen days sailing ahead of her.

From the 7th to the 13th almost continuous calm.

The 14th, at 9 o'clock we caught sight to the south of a ship which pursued us under full sail. At 6 o'clock he asked for our standard, launched his boat with an officer and ten men, who came aboard to examine our papers; we recognized him as the freebooter, commanded by Captain Taylor. After that, they re-embarked and set out in pursuit of a ship which was in sight to the northwest.

From the 15th to the 18th almost continual bad weather; nothing new; the 19th calm, west wind. During the day we harpooned several dolphins; and in the afternoon, as our captain was hurling his harpoon over the bowsprit he fell overboard; we succeeded in saving him. In the evening there were violent squalls.

From the 20th of September to the 12th of October nothing extraordinary happened; we experienced considerable bad weather; at 9 o'clock we threw out the lead which grounded in yellow sand at 35 fathoms. At 11 o'clock another sounding brought up mixed sand from 24 fathoms.

The 13th of October, west wind; took several soundings and found bottom at from 12 to 15 fathoms. In the afternoon we saluted an American schooner, *The Anna*, from Philadelphia bound for Providence.

On the 14th of October, wind N.N.W. At 6 o'clock in the morning it was with great pleasure that we saw land; tacked about during the remainder of the day before the entrance to the river; continuous sail; in the afternoon we reached the open sea.

The 15th, wind N.N.W. Weather fine. In the morning we steered for the river, and at 8 o'clock in the evening we saw the beacon; we hung out the signal-light, and shortly afterwards we had the pleasure of having a pilot on board; at eleven o'clock we anchored in the river on account of the bad weather.

On the 16th we sailed; fine weather; the captain with a passenger went ashore at New York and we headed for that city.

We arrived about one o'clock. New York is the first commercial city of the United States, and the best defended because of superb batteries established along the Hudson.

I remained ten days in New York, and then set out for Philadelphia, where, I had been told, I would find French people, and the leaders in the project to found the Texas colony. As soon as I arrived I presented myself to the Generals who were in command of the expedition. I was welcomed like a brother, like a friend. And during the month of November and the first days of December we all worked together, gathering what was necessary for the organization and establishment of the colony.

Chapter Second
VOYAGE FROM PHILADELPHIA TO GALVESTON
SOJOURN ON THAT ISLAND
DEPARTURE FOR CHAMP D'ASILE
OF A DETACHMENT OF A HUNDRED MEN
THEY LACK FOOD THEY EAT A POISONOUS HERB
THEY ESCAPE DEATH THROUGH THE HELP
OF AN INDIAN

SEVENTEENTH DECEMBER: WE
heaved anchor and set sail at ten o'clock in the morning,
with north winds, in the American schooner *Huntress*, under the command of Lieutenant-General Rigaud.

The same day, at two o'clock in the afternoon, we anchored in the river.

18. Set sail at 8 o'clock in the morning, and anchored at
2 o'clock in the sight of Newcastle.

19. Set sail at six o'clock in the morning, and entered
the open sea at eleven o'clock in the evening.

At ten o'clock an Italian servant of Colonel Jeannet fell
a victim to a cowardly assassination committed by some
rogues who had caused certain false suspicions to rest upon
him. As soon as we reached our destination, they were
expelled from the colony.

On the 20th, at one o'clock in the morning, we were surprised by a great tempest and were obliged to bring her head around. North wind.

On the 21st, same weather, and very cold; the whole crew had their hands and feet frozen; many of the ropes and irons of the rigging broke.

On the 22nd, at 10 o'clock in the morning, the weather began to clear, and all hands set about repairing the damages. Northwest winds.

The 23rd, fine weather, south wind.

From the 24th to the 27th, dead calm.

On the 28th there was a good breeze and we arrived in sight of the island of Abaco. On midnight of the 29th we arrived off the great Bahama Bank. On the 30th, at 10 o'clock in the morning, we had a three-masted American ship in view, which had run up its distress signal; we headed for it, and it launched its small boat. The second mate came aboard, and we learned that a tempest had cast them there, after having damaged their rudder and carried away several of their sails. For a week they had remained in this position, making the necessary repairs for the continuance of their voyage; they begged us to make mention of this in the newspapers as soon as we arrived. At 6 o'clock we anchored, for fear of going on the rocks. On the 31st, at 5 o'clock in the morning, we set sail with a west wind; in the evening, dead calm.

On the 1st of January, 1818, a dead calm, and the sun rose radiant.

On the 2nd, at one o'clock in the morning, we passed the Bahama Bank; north wind; the rest of the night, calm; at 5 o'clock in the morning a slight breeze came up and we saw shortly afterwards the shores of the island of Culo; the weather was very warm; at 6 o'clock in the evening, in sight of Havana, stormy weather. On the 4th we lost sight of Havana, and at 6 o'clock we saw the Island of the Turtles. North wind.

From the 5th to the 7th, nothing new, same weather, in the evening except that on the 7th we had a violent storm.

From the 8th to the 13th, west wind and several squalls.

On the 14th, at 10 o'clock in the morning, we saw a ship to the northwest, which we recognized as a brig, heading for us; at 4 o'clock in the evening it ran up a Spanish flag and launched its small boat, carrying an officer and four men. When it had drawn alongside of us, we learned that it was a prize taken from the Spaniards by the freebooter Couleuvre, and that it was bound for Galveston. The captain begged us to let him have some biscuit and tobacco; in exchange he gave us Spanish wines, figs, oil, olives, etc.

On the 15th, calm; at 8 o'clock the Spanish prize sent us her skiff with various refreshments; in the evening a good breeze, still sailing together.

The 16th, south wind, sailing northwest. It was with great pleasure that we caught sight of Galveston at 8 o'clock in the morning. At 11 o'clock we anchored in the roadstead, in seven fathoms of water. At noon the pilot came aboard to take us into the harbor. At 3 o'clock we went aground on a bank where we were obliged to anchor and wait for the tide. General Rigaud, accompanied by Messrs. Douarches, Jeannet, Schultz, Hartmann, Groningue, got into the boat to go ashore to find Sieur Lafitte, owner of independent Mexican corsairs, acting in capacity of governor, to insure the safety of our debarkation and the establishment of our provisional camp.

From the 17th to the 18th, in the roads. At noon M. Lafitte came on board; we succeeded in getting afloat, and the landing was accomplished. At 2 o'clock in the afternoon we busied ourselves in constructing a camp to shelter us from the inclemencies of the weather during our sojourn in this desert island. Galveston is an island occupied by independent Mexicans; there is not a single tree to be found,* in consequence, apparently, of the floods to which the island is often exposed, being almost on sea-level. Properly speaking, it is only a calling port for the vessels which want to cast anchor in the bay, to cruise about or to make repairs.

We remained on this island until the beginning of March and during that time lived by fishing and hunting, in order to economize in our provisions and salt meats.

The first days of March were of good augury for us. General Charles Lallemand, head of the colony, arrived with a great many other colonists. Joy reigned among us; we forgot our weariness and our misfortunes and gave a little party, such as was permitted by circumstances and our situation. Gaiety, frankness and sweet out-pourings of friendship characterized our celebration in place of the luxury, extravagance and envy which make European gatherings so fastidious. Patriotic songs resounded; we drank to the happiness of our dear fatherland, to our friends who still lived there, to our good fortune, to the success of our undertaking, and to the prosperity of the colony we were founding.

On the 10th of March, in the evening, we embarked, and it was agreed that we should meet at the head of the bay. Our little fleet was composed of 24 ships; scarcely had we reached the open bay when a very violent storm arose and

* In the margin a hand-written note says there are four plum-trees.

scattered us. The darkness of night made our situation still more critical; several of the boats leaked badly, and were for a long time on the point of being swallowed up. The greater number of the boats arrived, however, without accident at the place appointed for the meeting, and we were careful to light fires in order to rally those which were still separated from us. Unfortunately, the ship on which were our brave comrades Schultz, Larochette, Hartmann, Rieffel, Monnot, Fallot, Bontoux and Gilbal was delayed longer than the others. She was leaking so badly they were obliged to throw overboard the provisions they carried, as well as their baggage; in fact, everything they had, in order to empty the water which was pouring in.

The seas being very high, they expected every moment to founder; undoubtedly they would have done so if they had not had the good fortune to touch on a little shoal, where they remained until midnight. Relief came to them from Galveston, our friends there having heard the cannon shots which they (the crew) continued to fire as a signal of distress; fortunately they all were saved.

Another boat on which were our unfortunate companions Majors Voerster, Genait, Ferlin, Meunier le Rhonuillet, and the major's servant, was not so fortunate. The waves sank it soon after its departure. Sieur Genait was the only one who escaped. After swimming for three hours, he succeeded in reaching the bay, where, overcome with weariness, and half dead, he found a little sand bank where he rested. It is difficult to express the grief we felt on learning of this misfortune. Sincere tears fell for our companions; each of us mourned among them a friend and brother; we were all one family. How eloquent our grief was! What a funeral oration was the praise which we accorded those whom the tempest had torn from us! All had given proof of courage, devotion, and bravery, and had a hundred times braved death on the battlefield; the sea ended their careers, just as they expected to find rest and forget the injustice of Fate in friendships and in the fairest and purest enjoyments. It is thus that Fortune laughs at our plans. She shows us a brilliant future; our eyes are fixed upon the picture; we advance, little heeding the abyss which is beneath our steps; it engulfs us, and there is life and the span of our hopes: Poor mortals! Why dream so many dreams?

On the 11th in the morning, as soon as all the boats were united, we set sail in fine weather, and in the evening all pitched camp near Red-fish Bank.

On the 12th and 13th, bad weather and rain did not permit us to continue our way. These two days seemed interminable to us. It was impossible to give ourselves up to hunting and fishing, the only amusements offered us; and, although there were so many of us that conversation should not have been lacking, it often languished. Some amongst us, however, had the talent of renewing it by their gaiety and witty words.

It was not until the morning of the 14th that we set out. We arrived at what is known as Perrey Point. where we camped until the morning of the 16th. Generals Lallemand and Rigaud then decided to go on foot to Champ d'Asile situated near the Trinity River, at about 20 leagues from the Gulf of Mexico, and they set out with a detachment of a hundred men; the remainder were left to find the river, and bring up the supplies and ammunition, under the orders of Colonel Sarrazin, who thought we were perfectly familiar with the river's mouth.

We expected to arrive at our destination and rejoin our companions on the following day. Unfortunately this hope was not realized, and our luckless comrades were on the point of falling victims to the delay.

They had taken provisions for only two days; on the third and the fourth, hunger made itself felt desperately, and each sought means of satisfying it. It was thought that a precious and healthful discovery had been made in a plant which looked much like lettuce. It was cooked and eaten; scarcely was this done when the dangerous results were felt —it was a violent poison. A half-hour after this fatal meal all those who had partaken of it lay stretched upon the ground, wracked by the most terrible convulsions. Generals Lallemand and Rigaud and Surgeon Mann were not stricken with this illness, for, although tormented by hunger, they had been prudent enough not to taste the venomous herbs.

It is impossible to describe the frightful predicament in which they found themselves. Surrounded by ninety-seven bodies whose distorted features threatened early death, they were unable to do anything toward relief, for the supply of medicine had been left on the ships. What could they do? What was to become of them? What resolution was there to take? In the new world the antidote grows beside its poison; but how could it be found, and how were they to know it? Those are the questions Generals Lallemand and Rigaud, and Dr. Mann asked themselves.

In this state of anxiety they were prey to the darkest reflections, when chance, or rather an unexpected piece of luck, led thither an Indian of the *Cochatis* tribe. He was a good angel sent by Providence to snatch our friends from the death threatening them. He is surprised to see them in that state; he is shown the plant which caused the misadventure; he raises his hands and his eyes toward heaven, utters a sad cry, leaves with the swiftness of lightning and returns a few moments after with some plants he has gathered. These were boiled according to his directions, and then, with the aid of a piece of wood used to open the mouths of the poison victims, each one was made to drink a potion; soon afterwards they regained consciousness, and came entirely to themselves. They still suffered, however, for several days from their imprudence; but they experienced in the end no bad results.

It is easy to imagine our gratitude to the good, kind savage who appeared to attach no importance to the service he rendered us. This humane act seemed quite a natural thing to him. What an example this Indian is for civilized peoples. It is rather the instinct of nature which leads us to virtue, to kindheartedness than all the highly wrought precepts of conscious eloquence. Words escape from the mouth; but the desire, the wish to put them in practice, does not always move the heart to action. Good savage! The name of this nation shall never leave my memory. The refugees of Champ d'Asile raise an enduring monument to you in their hearts; it is based on thankfulness and friendship. We have Gallicized many words which do not produce so vivid an image as that of *Cochatis;* and we wish that to everyone it might become the symbol of kindness and humanity.

Our readers will be glad to pardon us this digression in behalf of this motive of humanity. If the beginnings of our misfortunes have interested them, they cannot be insensible to the expressions of our gratitude.

Chapter Three
ARRIVAL OF THE SHIPS IN TEXAS
REUNION OF ALL THE COLONISTS
ESTABLISHMENT OF THE CAMP AND THE FORTIFICATIONS
ORGANIZATION AND FORMATION OF THE TROOPS
PROCLAMATION OF GENERAL LALLEMAND

IT WAS NOT UNTIL THE SIXTH day after their departure that the boats joined the detachment which had gone on foot to Champ d'Asile, arriving at the camp which had been established on the banks of the Trinty. They had gone too far out to sea and had not immediately found the mouth of the river. This delay, as has been seen, subjected us to the greatest misfortunes, particularly in a wild, uncivilized country, all of whose products —by the test we had made of them—seemed poisonous. On their side, our comrades were not less troubled about our fate; they knew we had supplies for two days only, and that famine would soon assail us. We had accused them, for misfortune makes people unjust and suspicious—little amenable to mature consideration. All we could do was encourage each other to resignation. Some among us, and they were in the majority, displayed great strength of character, proving that adversity could not dismay them. The silence that reigned and the morose expression of every one gave evidence of the feeling to which our spirits had fallen prey. Generals Lallemand and Rigaud, setting an example of fortitude, consoled us and kept our hopes alive; but words are necessarily feeble shifts against misfortune. Finally the arrival of the vessels restored us to plenty. An account of what we had gone through made our comrades shudder. We soon forgot our griefs upon the breast of friendship, and the past was no longer anything but a dream.

As soon as provisions, supplies, and other necessities were unloaded we busied ourselves with laying out a provisional camp and providing shelter from the vagaries of the weather. Next we were organized into troops, Generals Lallemand and Rigaud naming the leaders. Once this organization was completed, the plans of four forts were outlined. The first, situated on the right of the camp, was called *Fort Charles*, from the name of the General-in-Chief; the second, *Middle Fort*; the third, *Fort Henry*, which was on the left and communicated by a covered roadway with two guardhouses established in the camp. The fourth, placed to the right of the stockade of the camp, on the shores of the Trinity, defended the banks and covered the three other forts. It was called the *Fort of the Stockade*, and had three pieces of cannon. *Fort Charles* had two pieces; *Middle Fort* one; and *Fort Henry* two; in all, eight pieces of cannon formed our artillery.

Everyone set to work with the greatest industry. The Generals worked at our head, and General Rigaud, although in advanced years, gave way in nothing to the young men: He was to be seen with pick and spade in hand, never a moment idle, directing all of us. Working hours were set from 4 to 7 o'clock in the morning and from 4 to 7 in the after-

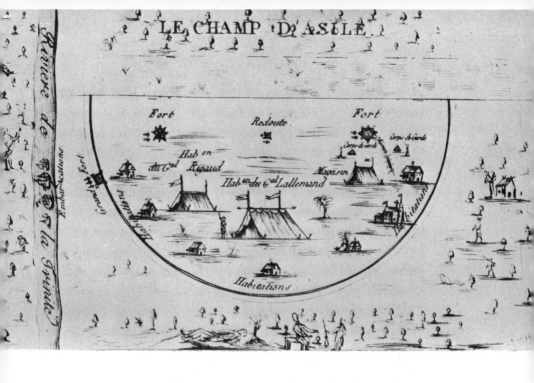

Diagram of Champ d'Asile

noon. Operations were directed by Messrs. Mauvais, Guillot, Arlot and Manscheski, artillery officers.

Between working hours each man might attend to the building of his own house or the cultivation of his garden.

In a very short space of time these forts were reared, as if by magic, and they were of astonishing strength. The principles of military science had been strictly adhered to, and the fortifications raised by the famous Vauban, or the best officers in the spirit of our times, could offer nothing better. We all consecrated to this work a certain amount of pride; and we were, so to speak, at once pioneers and engineers.

The *Stockade Fort* was built of great trees, and was so solid it could easily have held against any attack. The powder-magazines and the colony's supplies were deposited there. The private houses were laid out on a circular plan in a wide space above the forts. They were built of big trees joined together in block-house fashion, bulletproof and with loop-holes, so that each one would have to be attacked separately. In the rear center was General Lallemand's house; a little farther on, at the right, was the store-house. General Rigaud had his house above *Fort Henry*, near the two guard-houses. The *ensemble* view of the camp was very pleasing. This rustic and war-like picture had something charming about it which it is difficult to convey: before the camp a wide plain; behind it the thick evergreen trees, whose tops were lost, so to speak, in the clouds; to the right rolled the Trinity River, watering the borders of the colony, to lose itself in the Gulf of Mexico. On the far bank were forests stretching away as far as the eye could reach. The left and rear of the camp were sheltered by forests to protect us from tempests. This landscape, as can be understood, had about it something picturesque and majestic; to visualize it, one has only to glance at the map accompanying this work.

As we have already said, between working hours the colonists cultivated their gardens, and the very fertile soil responded to our labor. Vegetation was rank, and the earth was soon covered with plants and fruits. Messrs. Hartmann and Fux were the first who had fruit. The melons especially were of rare beauty and extraordinary size; as were all the plants set out in the earth—it gave us back with interest everything we confided to its bosom. It seemed that it was trying to recompense us by its abundant yield for our separation from the fatherland, and repay us for our choosing it as a place of refuge.

We had also made several plantings of Naquidoche, which did very well; but we did not stay long enough in the country to reap the fruits of our labors. I am persuaded that tobacco would eventually have been a very resourceful branch of industry for the colony if we had given more extensive care to its culture.

The greatest order and unity reigned in the colony. We followed the civil and military regulations in force in France. We think we should insert here the Proclamation that General Lallemand put into effect some days after our arrival. It will make known our aims and the principles of conduct which animated us.

* * *

PROCLAMATION

At Galveston the—

"Brought together by a series of misfortunes which exiled us from our homes and scattered us abroad in various countries, we are resolved to seek an asylum where we can remember our misfortunes to profit thereby. A great country stretches out before us, uninhabited by civilized man, given over to Indian tribes who do naught but hunt, leaving idle a territory as fertile as extensive. In adversity, far from being subdued in courage, we are exercising the first right given by the Author of Nature, that of settling on this earth, to cultivate it, and draw from it the products which nature never refused to the patient laborer.

"We are attacking no one, and we have no hostile intentions. We ask peace and friendship with all around us, and we shall be grateful for their good will. We shall respect the religion, laws, customs, and usages of civilized nations. We shall respect the independence, practices and mode of life of the Indian tribes, whom we shall trouble neither in the hunt nor in the exercise of any other of their pursuits. We shall establish social and neighborly, as well as commercial, relations with all those whom such intercourse will please. Our conduct will be peaceable, active, and industrious. We shall be as useful as we can, and we shall return good for good; but if it be possible that our position is not respected, if persecution should fall upon us in the wilderness where we have sought retreat, we ask all civilized men if we are not justified in defending ourselves with the greatest devotion. Our decision is made in advance: we have arms; the necessity of self-preservation led us to provide ourselves with these, just as men in our position have always done. The land upon which we have established ourselves will see us succeed or die. Here it is our desire to live in a free and honorable way, or here find our grave, and just men will accord a tribute of esteem to our memory.

"But we have come here for a happier fate, and our first care must be to merit general approbation by laying down the principles which shall regulate our conduct. We shall call our colony Champ d'Asile. This name, while reminding us of our adversities, will remind us also of the necessity of providing for the future, of establishing new homes —in short, of creating a new fatherland. The colony, essentially agricultural and commercial, will be military for its defense; and it will be divided into cohorts; each troop will have a leader who will be expected to keep a register. A general register, composed of the combined registers of all the troops, will be kept in the central depot of the colony. The cohorts will be gathered on the same spot for better protection from attack, and each will live peaceably under the eye of authority. A code will be drawn up immediately to secure the safety of property and liberty of persons, to prevent and suppress injustice, to insure peace among the well-disposed, and to defeat the schemes of the wicked.

"The refugees will admit to their group only French people or soldiers who have served in the French Army. To join them it is enough to possess one of these two qualifications and to go to New Orleans, where applicants will find everything in readiness to conduct them to Champ d'Asile and admit them to the colony."

* * *

134

Work was done with the greatest punctuality, and discipline rigorously adhered to, obedience and subordination constituting the foundation of our society.

One spirit animated us all, and held us to the same objective: the prosperity of the colony, its growth and general security, and the well-being of each individual in it. There was no jealousy, no unworthy ambition among us; corrupting luxury did not tempt us. Our arms were our jewels; our land, homes, and gardens our wealth. The fruits the earth gave us and our farming instruments were all means of diversion. Everything was shared amongst us; and if sickness happened to strike down one of our brothers, he was given the promptest relief that solicitude, attention, and aid could afford. Interchange of sympathy, reciprocity of delicate actions, proofs of friendship, interest, and attachment strengthened moment by moment the bonds binding us to each other. Such, in general, are all early societies. Why are they not still in their dawn? Cruel dissensions, children of passion, would not come to trouble their peace and harmony. We were living on a new soil, and we seemed, so to speak, to enjoy the same advantages. The air we breathed was purer, it affected our vitals, it reacted on us for good: corruption and such ideas as one finds in great societies in the heart of cities left us; and, like nature which presented itself to our eyes, we felt ourselves without the vices and mistakes that affect humanity and constitute man's misfortune. It was common needs that drew us together; and the work which we were obliged to do did not allow us to give ourselves up to other thoughts. I think, rather I am certain, that idleness is the greatest of scourges, and I recognize that a hard-working people whose principal source of wealth is industry is less liable than any other to suffer a breakdown of morals; that it counts among its members more good fathers and good citizens, virtuous sons, and friends of humanity than those societies which are gorged with gold, whose delight is luxury. It is this sinister metal which gives birth to crimes, and we had brought none to Texas.

Our colony was composed of four hundred individuals of various nations. I include in the cohorts that I append only Frenchmen and a few high Spanish officers who were members of the colony until our departure.

* * *

DIVISION OF THE COHORTS
General Staff
Messrs. Lallemand, General and Commander-in-Chief; Rigaud, General and Second in Command.

First Cohort
Messrs. Colonel Douarche, *chief;* Waskès, Spanish Colonel; Lapeire, *dead*; Gazola; Schmids; Contardie; Pagnère, André; Paguère, Alexandre; Mollina; Tournel; Skierdo; François, Schmids, L.; Peugné; Joseph Merlin, *drowned*; Moeller; Didier; Baron; Gibal; Plauque, Sr.; Plauque, Jr.; Methais; La Rouillet, *drowned*; Deseorme; Allouard; Stephens; Lejune, *drowned*; Manuel; Wallot; Schumps; Corso; Planté; Prolmés; Genait; Meunier, *drowned*; Gex; Edmond-Dreux; Ouzard; Salanav; Aimard; Gonzoles; Salaza; Toubaux; Félix; Blanck; Hudbert; Normann; Neschberg, *dead*; Sudermann, *dead*; Schumpin; Frederick; Delfund; Durand,

ex-receiver general; Buillard, *surgeon of the first cohort;* Viol, *doctor.*

Second Cohort

Messrs. Colonel Scharassin, *chief;* Schultz; Jourdan, *dead;* Jeannet; Fischer; Delfoss; Rigaud, *son of the general;* Voerster, *drowned;* Hartmann, Larochette; Bieffel; Arander; Fux; Canobiou; Bischoff; Farcy; Fallot, *devoured by savages;* Balbuena; Goméz; Mony; Latapie; Ruger; Astorge; Schrimer; Galland, *dead;* Houdard; Artus; Manfretty; Penazzi; Desplans; Vinet, Lacoste; Jeannet, Joseph; Bonnet; Barrault; Laurette; Peygnére; Monier; Ferlin, *drowned;* Etienne; Beauvais; Descoudréz; Barillier; Renoud; Labordet; Lagrade; Albert, *devoured by savages;* Hebert; Millard; Pomier; Loubrault; Lagage; Baudel; Rub; Durand; Frédéric; Lagarde; Monnot, *surgeon of the second cohort.*

Third Cohort

Messrs. Colonel Fournie, *chief;* Guillot; Germain; Manschesky; Maillet; Holzer; Vitalba; Torta; Richard; Bontoux, *dead;* Dejean, *clothing officer;* Lafeuillade; Lange; Laurent; Groningue; Riban; Mauvais; Arlot; Boril; Dufot; Mann, *surgeon of the third cohort;* Formento, *chief doctor;* Jeannet, *uncle;* Manchot.

Names of Women and Children

Mesdames Jeannet and her son; Viol; Dejean with three children; Rigaud, daughter of the General.

* * *

We enjoyed the greatest tranquillity; deep peace surrounded us, calm and satisfaction reigned in all hearts; our camp was sacred ground where the golden age was to be born again.

It was there that we spent our days; it was within that enclosure that we gave ourselves up to the fondest hopes. They showed us the happiest future. The land enriched through our effort was soon covered with the most bountiful harvests; we tasted in advance the joys that one experiences when it can be said that everything before us is our work, the fruit of our labor and our steadfastness. Our imagination carried us back to our country, and we said with a certain pride, that when France has learned that her sons have made a settlement on unknown shores, where, one might say, no man's footprint had been left, she will be proud, proud of what we shall have done to stay adversity and defeat the harshness of Fate. She will recognize that no aspect of glory is foreign to us, and that these same men, who have distinguished themselves on the Champ de Mars and gathered there unnumbered laurels can also distinguish themselves by their industry. Commerce opened its resources to us; ships of the different nations plowing the waves of the Gulf would call at Champ d'Asile, bringing the products of Europe to exchange for those of Texas; and the French flag would wave in peace in the harbor of a new colony, next to that of nations that formerly were our rivals but will no longer feel anything but friendliness. Such were the thoughts which occupied our minds during our labors, and which we exchanged during moments of repose.

We thought ourselves safe from all reverses of Fortune, from all the blows of Fate. We were now inhabitants of a country whose concession had been made to us by a friendly people, who, like us, had passed through every hardship,

138

whose cradle of liberty had been encompassed with misfortune, and who each day saw its wealth and power increase, thanks to that cherished liberty, wise and tempered, whose fountain-head was in their laws and their strict observance. We could but believe that under the same sky, in the same climate, in taking as a model in everything the people who gave us hospitality, the same blessing would attend us.

But our first steps in the new career which we were to pursue were destined to be uncertain ones. Our first efforts in agriculture left much to be desired. Still novices, and living in a climate where the products of the soil and the methods of cultivation were different from those of our native country, we needed to be guided and instructed. The experience we might acquire by working was our only guide, and we our own teacher in this, the first of the arts, with which *Cincinnatus* and other men whose names history has handed down to us, occupied themselves after having gloriously served their countries.

We do not pretend to compare ourselves to those benefactors of mankind, to those heroes, to those citizen-warriors who, after the gods, worshipped only their country; but, without claiming to approach them, we were permitted to tread, though at a distance, in their footsteps. Our readers will see that we did not wish to give umbrage to anyone. Our plans, our desires, did not extend beyond the confines of our camp; it was our universe. Fishing and hunting were our favorite occupations when we wished to find diversion from other work. Living peacefully on the banks of the Trinity, we went with a treacherous hook, to try to beguile the water-folk in their deep caves. The fish that we took oftenest was the *coadfish;* we could also supply ourselves with turtles

139

—they were numerous there—very large, some of them weighed as much as two hundred pounds.

There were also many alligators, or crocodiles, in the Trinity River, and gars, fifteen to sixteen feet long and two to three feet broad, of which we caught a great many. They have jaws armed with teeth like our pike, but were of enormous size. Their skin was as thick and strong as a coat of mail. It was, as can be seen, dangerous to bathe in this river.

The country was surrounded by numerous lakes, and in them we angled for all kinds of fish, such as are found in the rivers of Europe.

Hunting, which was a much more active occupation, led us in pursuit of bear, roe-buck, deer and other animals. The hides of the former covered our beds and the flesh of the latter provided us with healthful and agreeable food. We were much like pastoral people in the first ages of the world, and the success of our hunting and fishing constituted the burden of our talk. Several among us were very skillful, being acquainted with all the tricks of the trade while we taught to the less experienced. When we did not succeed in getting the four-footed beasts or the birds of the air with our deadly lead, we set traps for them, and it was an additional delight to us, when, our appetites whetted by an unsuccessful shot, we would find them caught in our traps.

In the center of the camps where we lived, we were accustomed at times to disport ourselves in those games which tended to develop muscular strength, agility, and suppleness and skill of the body. The echoes of Texas resounded also with our songs; love and glory were celebrated; and the God of Wine—that conqueror of the Indies—was not forgotten.

It would seem I had lost my national character if I did not render homage to the ladies who had followed our fortunes and were the ornament of our society and the charm of the colony, who won the respect and admiration of all of us by those precious qualities so peculiarly their own. Good, kind, and sensible, attentive to everyone, conferring those delicate attentions of which women alone are capable, they ministered to the sick, and the sweet tones of their enchanting voices soothed the pain of the stricken. The remedies they offered, prepared by their own hands, seemed to acquire an added efficacy, a more precious quality, and thus to hasten recovery. In ages past, in times when mythology and its brilliant dreams charmed the Greeks, they would have been called dryads, hamadryads, nymphs. In our day they were ministering angels, virtuous women—in short, French women; and this word is the synonym of amiability, grace, talent, and all that can please and delight. Mademoiselle Rigaud was notable for her tender attachment to her father; she was a model of piety and filial love. One could not set eyes on her without finding himself better, without feeling the desire to be like her, without resolving to imitate her.

These ladies took part in our games and in our meetings which they ornamented; they came to visit us while we were at work; they applauded our success, our efforts, our perseverance. We were content with having won a word of praise and approval. We gave them flowers which we cultivated with care, that we might frequently renew these offerings. There were also several children among the colonists; and their careless joy gave variety to the picture. All the colonists cherished them, having an affection for them which was similar to the respect and deference accorded the ladies. Not one word was said which might have offended the most sensitive ear; a careless expression was frowned upon and forbidden to the language of the colony; and, while the ladies were present, nothing disturbed the charm and peace of our meetings. We imposed this rule upon ourselves, each individual voluntarily. Such is the Frenchman; it can be said without fear of contradiction that he has a good disposition and a kind nature, and that there is no good that he is not capable of, for he has only to follow the impulses of his heart.

Each one of us hastened to offer his services in beautifying or adding some new comfort to the dwellings of these ladies: one would work the garden, pull up the weeds, water the plants; another would tie up a flower whose stem was bent to the ground and destroy the insects on its petals. A smile, a word of thanks, a kind look was the reward for this slight service, and we were happy. Love, that sentiment which engenders in us a feeling Frenchmen adore, did not trouble us: if we did not know its pleasure, we were also strangers to its pains. We had, however, under our gaze two members of our colony whom the truest and sincerest love bound together in the tenderest ties. They loved each other to idolatry. All the colonists regarded them with an envying eye, but without jealousy. Who would not have longed to enjoy such fortune?

Nature seemed to have formed them for each other. What woman could be compared to the good, the sensible Adrienne? Where could be found her grace, her charm, her wit, this perfect union of gifts? What man would not have liked to resemble Edward? The most noble exterior was

142

the least of his good qualities: brave, generous, frank, loyal, a faithful friend, he loved his country and his brothers as much as he adored Adrienne. They lived together in the most beautiful union; all was happiness for them; they shared their pains and their pleasures, thus lightening the first, and sweetening the second. Happy lovers, I shall devote several pages of this work to a story of your love. You gave me your friendship. How many times was my heart moved at seeing the happy concord which reigned between you, which no cloud ever overshadowed! Adrienne, you whose name I cannot pronounce without experiencing the sweetest emotion! How many charming and loving women could be made up of the rare and precious qualities you combined in one rare creation. Shall I draw this picture? No, I shall only sketch it, and I am certain, thanks to the subject, that it will interest my readers.

At peace for the present, possessing almost everything necessary to our first needs, we saw the future in the most smiling light. After having made sure of our safety, we were about to break the ground, furrow the still virgin soil with the share and the plow, and confine to its bosom those nourishing seeds which in bountiful harvests would soon give us back a hundredfold that which we had confided to it—here a field of wheat, or barley, or corn; there the nourishing and useful potato and those other precious foods which were to keep us from hunger and famine. Alas! As we were cherishing these rosy hopes, we little thought that the dread scourge of famine with all its horrors was hovering over our heads about to strike us!

Chapter Four
SEVERAL INDIAN NATIONS SEND US ENVOYS
AND FORM A SORT OF ALLIANCE WITH US
THE PEACE OF THE COLONY IS DISTURBED
THE SPANIARDS FORMING THE GARRISONS OF
SAN ANTONIO AND LABADIE, JOINED WITH
THE INDIANS, DECIDE TO ATTACK US
WE FALL BACK UPON GALVESTON

THE COLONY, AS ONE SEES, could but become more and more prosperous, for the Indian tribes which adjoined us felt that they had nothing to fear from us and asked only to live on good terms with us, sending a deputation to offer us the *Peace Pipe* and pay their respects to General Lallemand. We received them heartily and our frankness and sincerity, that open-handed manner which characterizes the French, won their affection. A certain sympathy had at the first drawn us together, and the sincerest and truest attachment soon united us. You French, who will read this, imperfect as it is, will be moved by this touching picture of fraternity. The *Chactas*, the *Cochatis*, the *Alabamos*, the *Dankaves* were those who contracted alliances with us. These kind Indians admired our arms, of whose terrible use they were ignorant, not suspecting that their bows and arrows and tomahawks, were powerless against the flaming salt-petre and the dread *bayon-nette* which were always victorious in the hands of the French. They found some similarity between our dwellings and their wigwams, and we could see that they spoke of this among themselves.

They gave us presents, in return for which we presented them with certain trifles to which they seemed to attach considerable value. They left, after having assured us of their friendliness, with demonstrations which were the more to be prized because of their sincerity, for they smacked not at all of Europe with its falseness and clap-trap.

We thought, naturally enough, from this, that being on peaceful terms with the natives, we would have nothing to fear from the Europeans, who like us, were living in this region *without any other property title.*

How great was our error! For soon we learned that the Spanish garrisons of San Antonio, La Badie, La Bahia and La Bexar, with several partisan Indian tribes, were marching against us for the purpose of forcing us to abandon the province of Texas, as well as Champ d'Asile and Galveston Island. Although we were not numerous, we were accustomed to fight and to count our enemies after defeating them. Our first impulse was to await them firmly and punish them for their boldness. But maturer consideration tempered the first impulse of outraged courage, and our General pointed out the fact that our provisions might give out; and that after we had beaten the advance bands reinforcements would certainly come up to besiege our camp, reducing us to surrender or starvation. He counselled that the wisest and most prudent step would be to vacate Champ d'Asile and fall back upon Galveston, the only place where we could secure provisions because there we maintained communication by sea.

We all agreed with our General, whose wisdom and caution we had proved. We transported our provisions, supplies, and baggage to the boats which rode at anchor in the Trinity, and, after having bade adieu to our dwellings and to this Champ d'Asile where we had scarcely had time to establish our fireside gods, we embarked on the Trinity, whose current soon carried us into Galveston Bay.

Our retirement was accomplished in absolute order, without confusion or accident. One negro alone was drowned in spite of every effort to save him, carried away by the current. We also had Mr. Lejeune to regret, a naval officer, who was sent to Galveston three days before our departure to make necessary preparations for our arrival, and who had the misfortune to be drowned. This young sailor was remarkable for his earnestness, his activity and his personal qualities, and his loss was keenly felt by all the colonists, who missed him greatly.

Chapter Five

ARRIVAL AT GALVESTON; A NEW CAMP IS BUILT
THE OLD ONE HAVING BEEN BURNED
BREASTWORKS ARE THROWN UP
IT IS FEARED THE PROVISIONS MAY BE EXHAUSTED
GENERAL LALLEMAND LEAVES FOR NEW ORLEANS
TO PROCURE SUPPLIES THERE
THE SPANIARDS SEND US AN ORDER
TO EVACUATE GALVESTON

WE HAD A FORTUNATE SAIL ON the *Trinity*, arriving at Galveston where debarkation was soon accomplished. The camp we formerly occupied having been burned, we hurried to lay out another and were soon established in it. In order to insure ourselves against the assaults of those who might again wish to harass us, we threw up entrenchments, and placed our artillery upon them. Having taken these preliminary steps, we thought of consolidating the establishment until such time as we should reach a final decision as to the fate of the colony, or until we should go to a place from which we would not again be forced to retire.

The Spanish and the Indians would most certainly not have been able to force us to leave Champ d'Asile and Galveston Island if we had not been reduced to the direst want, and abandoned, so to speak, by the whole universe. Our arms

149

and, what is more, our courage would have furnished us the means of annihilating these insolent trouble-hunters. They would have learned that the French established in the New World were of that same stock which won laurels in every country of Europe. But let us not go too fast.

Security reigned among us, and if we did not have an actual abundance, neither did we fear want, and each man devoted himself to his own occupations, and performed his service, hunting or fishing. The days sped by, one much like the other.

Suddenly a sinister cry was heard—precursor of misfortune. The provisions were giving out; and the terrible truth of this alarm was too easily verified. Although our rations were reduced, we did not lose heart. Help was promised us; and we knew that a merchant had agreed to secure supplies for us. This consoling thought sweetened the bitterness of our privations and made them more bearable. Until such time as these promises should be kept, the General-in-Charge, whose strength and courage seemed to increase in proportion as our resources diminished, imbued every one with a confidence and hopes which he could not himself have, for we were now, each man, receiving only two biscuits and a small glass of *eaude vin*. Thus a month went by. All of us suffered more or less, and the work did not go on with the same industry. Although happiness did not reign in our colony there were, nevertheless, occasional flashes of it. Not a murmur, not a complaint was heard. Even the women displayed a courage and spirit which astonished us and evoked our admiration. Our respect and attachment for them grew hourly, and we are forced to admit that the so-called weaker sex possessed a strength which at times abandoned us.

We consoled each other as best we could, realizing the impossibility of securing any relief from Galveston Island, the soil being arid sand presenting the aspect of a desert; there was not a trace of vegetation, and the lapping of the waves and the whistling of the winds were the only sounds we heard. When for a moment we left our friends and the camp, nothing met the eye but the expanse of the Gulf, and if one saw a boat in the far distance, its course was eagerly followed until it was lost to sight and all hope of its being bound for Galveston was abandoned. Each vanishing hope made room for another, to be shattered in its turn. Such is man—he lives upon shadows, and, like the dog in the fable, he too often abandons a bone for a shadow.

The days flew by and still relief did not come. Anxiety was written on every face, which now bore traces of hunger—sinister forerunners of still graver misfortunes. But not a word was heard voicing the least discouragement, for who among us would have been the first to show less fortitude than his fellows? We were forced to decrease our rations still farther, and a fortnight passed in this terrible situation. We saw each day die with the hope that the morrow would better our lot: the dawn broke, and we still cherished the thought. Staring out to sea, we endeavored to descry the rescuing and protecting sail which, bellied by a favorable wind, would mean happiness and plenty for us once more. Vain hope! It was not to appear, for Destiny was deaf to our entreaties, and cruel Fate was to deliver us up to all the horrors of famine and despair.

At last General Lallemand, at his wit's end that the provision merchant did not keep his promises, decided, near the end of September, to go to New Orleans with a commissioner of the United States, Mr. Graham, who had come to Galveston. He hoped to be able there to secure relief and end our suffering; so he left, taking with him his *aides de camp*, together with seven or eight persons for an escort. Before his departure, he drew up an order in which he made it known that it grieved him to leave us, that his absence would not be prolonged, and that he was going only for our own good. He exhorted us to maintain order in the colony, saying that we would see him again within twenty or thirty days, and that he would send us supplies immediately—we scarcely had enough to last a month. He left General Rigaud in command. This respected soldier, aged about eighty* years, was loved by all the colonists, whom he regarded as his children, inspiring them with the greatest confidence.

We were not afraid of dying from hunger. Such an idea had never occurred to us, for accustomed as we were to the privations incident to sieges, we could but meet such trials with courage. The General's departure, however, caused a great sensation in camp, for there are certain emotions one cannot suppress, presentiments, which assail us in spite of ourselves, and against which it is impossible to protect one's self. We had the greatest respect for General Rigaud, and his cheering voice, his strength and his example put new courage into us. But when we thought of General Lallemand's departure, of its consequences, of the disasters which would ensue if help did not come, our hopes were dashed. Consternation held us all in its grip. Our misfortune seemed to have reached its height, and each man thought only of his personal safety and how to protect himself against hunger.

* A manuscript note in French in the margin of the book used for this translation gives his age as 58 years.

Want makes us hard and selfish, closes the heart to friend-ship and the tenderest affections—brings one to the last stages of suffering.

A canteen was established which still sold us certain poor supplies for gold, charging us twenty-five sous for a small glass of *eau de vin* and proportionate prices for other com-modities. Unfortunate indeed were those who had no money, and such was the plight of most of the colonists. Soon, as a last means of escaping starvation, we sold our possessions to the store-keeper, who gave us in exchange a piece of bread, diminished to the very limit in size by his avarice and greed for gain.

Are there then no countries on earth, no place of refuge for the unfortunate, where kind and compassionate men are to be found? The vices of civilization penetrate everywhere; in the heart of cities, in the midst of deserts, and in Texas; as well as on the banks of the Seine, one meets with degraded beings, who, to accumulate a little gold, will speculate on the misfortunes of their fellows.

All of these thoughts were ours, for we saw only want and sought only for some means of escaping from it. But we had not yet experienced all the blows misfortune had prepared for us. A few days after General Lallemand's departure, the Spanish Commissioner who had taken pos-session of Champ d'Asile after our departure, sent an envoy enjoining us to leave Galveston Island. This demand we re-fused, replying that we could make no such decision in the absence of the General-in-Chief, and that we would await his return or his orders to treat with them. At this the agent returned to Texas and we heard no more of him.

Chapter Six
MORE ACUTE LACK OF FOOD
NEW MISFORTUNES—TEMPEST—FLOOD
THE SEA BREAKS ITS BONDS
SUBMERGES A PART OF THE ISLAND
DESTROYS THE BUILDINGS, DRAGS AWAY OUR BOATS
AND OCCASIONS THE LOSS OF THE REMAINING FOOD
FRESH WATER LACKING
GENERAL RIGAUD'S SON IS SENT TO NEW ORLEANS
WHAT THE FLOOD DESTROYED IS REBUILT

THE SPANIARDS' ATTACK WAS
not what we feared most, for, if we but had the strength to
bear arms, we felt certain of victory. We preferred peace,
however, for we had learned by experience that success is
bought only at the cost of brave lives. A man's blood is precious, and the losses we would have undergone would have
been the greater to us, because of the affection that bound
us together: for one can hardly conceive of the dearness of
the bonds which united us. I am pleased to stress this thought
in order to remind my readers from time to time of a situation which could not fail to interest them.

Since our return to Galveston the sea had remained continually calm and serene, and the temperature pleasant. We
several times remarked that Fate was not entirely against us

and that, worn as we were with combating the forerunners of famine, what a great misfortune it would have been if we had been forced to struggle against inclement weather. We looked upon this boon as an omen foretelling that we were soon to be delivered from our straits. We had little idea that the storm was gathering about our heads and that all which had so far happened to us was as nothing compared to the new blows to be dealt by a Fate whose only function seemed to pursue us.

Just at nightfall we were gathered together in different portions of our camp, when the sky began to darken, the clouds to pile up, the wind to rise, and the sea-birds to seek shelter on the land. At last all the signs of an approaching tempest were observed, without fright, however, or the least misgiving, for we thought our camp would shelter us from the wind and our dwellings were, moreover, not high enough to offer much resistance to it. We had several times seen our camp tried, and did not now expect a storm of greater violence. We contented ourselves with strengthening the stakes which seemed weak and assured ourselves that our boats were safely moored. Night soon covered the land with its sable wings, and each man sought his humble abode, there to give himself up to sleep. Her poppies had weighted down our lids when, suddenly, a frightful noise aroused us from our dreams, and we heard the howling of the wind and the bellowing of the waves dashing wildly against our entrenchments. Flashes of lightning showed us the rampage of the heavens, which frightened us more than the darkness that surrounded us, and, although the danger had been very great before, it now seemed a thousand times greater.

Finally the sea burst its confines and inundated the island, rushing into camp and dwellings, submerging everything. Before long we found ourselves surrounded by water four feet deep. Consternation reigned: the cries of distress and pain could be heard amid this frightful chaos, soon to be drowned in the roaring of the waves and the screaming of the wind. It is easy to understand with what wild impatience and anxiety we waited for the daylight which must follow this terrible and eternal night, whose disaster our imagination must needs exaggerate.

At last came the light to show us our losses. With dreadful misgivings we looked about us, dreading to see what might meet our gaze, yet unable to restrain our curiosity. What a sad sight! It was a picture of Nature's destruction, when her laws seemed to have gone awry. The waves striking in all directions tossed beams and kegs about the ruined walls. Galveston village looked like a fort beaten down by assault. We gazed at each other without being able to make a move to improve our condition. The currents were so swift that it was impossible to stand against them.

We saw Adrienne and her husband, whose dwelling was somewhat removed from the others, struggling with the waves. Edward was clinging with his left arm to a heavy stake, tossed by the waters, and with the other was supporting his beloved, who, pale and lifeless, seemed to have thoughts only for him who forgot his own dangers in order to shield her from them. Dear pair, so worthy of the love and interest which we bore you! I reserve for the recital of your own misfortunes, an account of all that you suffered. This episode will affect all hearts, and quick tears will damp the eye of more than one reader, which will not spring from any charm of style; but when I shall have drawn Adrienne and Edward with life-like touches, who could feel anything but a great interest in them?

We had the vain hope that the wind would calm when day came, and the tempest become less violent. Of all the houses in Galveston six alone withstood the fury of the waves which we saw break against the walls of the hospital where our sick lay, and even penetrate within. We could not bear the sight, and, throwing ourselves into the water carried the helpless to higher ground, to the house of M. Lafitte, and it was well we did so, for in a short while the sea would have become their grave.

The waves grew higher and higher, showing us at every moment the extent of our losses. The ships had not been able to withstand the repeated attacks of the waves, but dragged their anchors and were out to the open sea.* Despairing cries broke simultaneously from us all, for we still had some provisions on several of the boats, which we could not hope to recover—our ill luck had reached its climax. Every man trembled for his life, and the instinct of self-preservation made us forget that life would become a burden if famine should strike us with all its frightful train. Love of life is man's first emotion, and several of us made our way to the higher portions of the island, while others climbed atop of buildings to escape the flood of waters surrounding us, leaving nothing to hope for. We could see death on all sides, and each said to the other that it was only a few moments away for us. We spent two days in this cruel position, but the third dawned fairer: the wind calmed, the waves sub-

* The private citizens, principally M. Lafitte, governor of the island, suffered considerable losses.

sided, the sky cleared: and towards evening we were able to come together, though the water still stood in pools about us.

We were indeed a pitiable sight. As each companion joined the group he was embraced all around, and every man told of the dangers he had sustained and of the hopes and fears that followed. After these first expressions of affection, we felt the need of restoring our strength. Hunger and thirst, those terrible scourges of humanity, tormented us, and, although we still had a little food, our tanks were filled with salt water. Fresh water was not to be found on the island, and we could hope for none from the mainland since we had lost our ships. We dug wells only to find that the sea-water had gone everywhere. Fortunately for us, some of the colonists had filled several barrels with fresh water before the storm, and this we divided equally, giving ourselves over to the hope that Providence would come to our relief.

Two days later, several of our men, in going about the island, seeking lost articles, discovered two of our boats, about six leagues inward. This was a precious discovery for us, for we were now able to go to the mainland and bring back enough water to last until our own cisterns should sweeten again.

Our provisions were exhausted, and it was impossible to procure more, for we were thirty or forty leagues from the nearest Indian settlement. We doubted if the Spanish, who had taken possession of Champ d'Asile after our departure, would come to our relief. In this uncertain state some decision had to be reached. We had to live, and we had to provide for the needs of our ill comrades, who were in no position to share our present misfortunes. Fishing and hunting became our only occupations, and we gave ourselves up to these with an ardor born of necessity and were happy to see success crown our efforts and perseverance. When we returned to camp from our forays, we would present to the ladies the game which seemed most worthy of them; and they would call us their providers, their true friends, and sympathize with us, regretting that we were obliged to give ourselves so much trouble. But the pleasure of serving our ladies made us forget our fatigues, and we would begin the following day with the same eagerness.

The hope of having news of our General, who had gone to New Orleans, still sustained us, and in order to hasten the help he had promised, several days after the unfortunate event which almost annihilated us, we sent General Rigaud's son on with news of what had happened. This excellent young man set out, attended by our good wishes and blessing. His father embraced him, his sister bade him a sad farewell, and he quitted the place which presented on all sides a picture of misery and desolation.

We maintained our courage, however, for it is in misfortune that one finds the strength to meet it and to show one's self superior to difficulties. Adversity had, so to speak, transformed our spirits and our dispositions; for there was not one among us who could be reproached for the slightest sign of weakness, and it was with a new-found ardor that we all prepared for work again. Gaiety soon resumed its sway, and to the singing of war songs, we rebuilt what the flood had destroyed; each, pick in hand, relating experiences under similar circumstances. One had seen a landslide on the Alps, the Simplon, or the St. Bernard passes. Another told what had happened in Italy when the Po overflowed and he nearly lost his life. A third spoke of the rampages of the Danube, whose flood, impossible to bridle, destroyed the bridges and nearly bottled up in the land of Lobau the conquerors of Austerlitz, Jena, Eylau, and Friedland.

"Well, my friends," added General Rigaud, "victory, which remained faithful to our flag, triumphed over all difficulties, and the enemy armies disappeared like thin mist before our invincible phalanxes. Success will crown our efforts also, and if we here do not have to fight the enemies of our country, we shall none the less triumph over the elements that wage war upon us, and we shall say with pride that, for a Frenchmen, everything is possible." A spontaneous bravo, and prolonged applause, carried far along the native shores, proved to our General that we shared his sentiments and would not lose heart.

We had but the bare necessities and were experiencing privations of many kinds; but we agreed among ourselves that it was possible to live on very little, and that man often made himself unhappy by creating fictitious needs for himself. What a school is misfortune! And what useful lessons it teaches! Happy the man who can turn them to account. This line of thought was certainly as good for us as any other. Our deputy was already gone thirty-two days and still we had no news. Not knowing what to think, we gave ourselves up to conjecture, but it was in vain that we sought to explain the causes of such cruel abandonment. It did not occur to us to accuse those who had always inspired us with so much confidence, who had given us such touching proofs of a sincere affection. Their truth, frankness, and loyalty, proven under divers circumstances, made us think that unforeseen difficulty, not to be charged to them, was the cause of the delay. In fact, how could we dream that a French General, whose fortunes we had followed, could be capable of deserting his companions in arms, when he knew them to be a prey to all the torments of dire necessity. Appearances, though often deceiving, led us to blame criminal neglect on the one whom our hearts took a certain pleasure in excusing; but when we looked about us, when we went over the past events, when we felt the anxieties of the moment, were we not also excusable for musing and trembling as to our future? It was this cruel expectancy which brought on a general discouragement, and made us resolve to flee from those lands which seemed to repel us and mark us with the seal of disapproval. We had to give up all the plans we had made; and those sweet dreams, children of the imagination, once so near to be realized, were now as the delusions of a delirium.

Some wanted to join the settlement on the island, others wanted to go to New Orleans, while still others thought of other American cities. France was the objective of most, with whose climate, fertility, and resources Champ d'Asile could scarcely compare; the latter place, moreover, had almost been our tomb. From that time on every man was actuated by only one notion: to prepare to leave the island.

Chapter Seven
WE LEAVE GALVESTON ISLAND
SOME, AFTER HAVING CROSSED THE BAY, GO TO LOUISIANA,
OTHERS TO NEW ORLEANS
A SMALL NUMBER EMBARK, THANKS TO M. LAFITTE,
WHO, IN SPITE OF THE LOSSES HE EXPERIENCED,
CAME TO OUR RESCUE

WE HAD TO LEAVE GALVESTON Island or die of hunger and misery; we chose the former. We did not have enough ships to go to New Orleans by water, or provisions enough for the voyage; neither could M. Lafitte, a resident of Galveston Island, fitter-out of independent Mexican corsairs, who up to that time had rendered us the greatest services, continue his help, despite his kind desires. The cyclone and flood had cost him two brigs, three schooners, and one sloop. The majority of us decided to go to the mainland, and thence overland to certain settlements where subsistence could be secured; and New Orleans was named as the general meeting-place. The unfortunate colonists were then carried across Galveston Bay to the land which was to have been their home, and each one set out in the direction he had previously fixed upon. Some, after crossing Texas, went to Alexandria, Louisiana, on the Red River; while others went to Nacogdoches, above

Lakes Pisaqui and Beshonneau, being attracted to this country by its reputation for fertility. Still others, having crossed the Sabine, the Carcassiou, and the Mermentas Rivers, traversed the country of the Attacapas and the Opelousas crossed the River Aux Boefs, and skirted the banks of Lake Barataria, they headed for New Orleans. During a journey of about 150 leagues they lived solely by hunting, finding habitations only at distances of two and three days' march. The people, who were for the most part Creole and French, welcomed them and gave them hospitality; but they were themselves too poor to furnish supplies, and had to content themselves with short periods of entertainment. Finally, after suffering infinite pains and great fatigue, they reached New Orleans, where they were the object of the most lively interest. The people of New Orleans did not seek to console them with pity but thought it a duty to heap upon them everything their sad plight demanded, for kindness ruled every heart.

M. Lafitte, despite the considerable sums owed him by the General-in-Chief, did not limit his generosity, but made still another sacrifice for the benefit of those who remained in Galveston, of whom I was one. He gave us, as means of conveyance to New Orleans, the sloop *St. Antonio de Campeche*, a Spanish prize, taken from that nation by one of the freebooters.

Placing aboard the supplies which he could spare us, and taking with us a captain and six Spanish sailors, whose liberty he restored, we set sail. Unfortunately we met contrary winds, and the food was about to give out completely when, after twenty days sailing, we sighted La Balise at the mouth of the Mississippi. Ascending the river, we were reunited with our comrades who had preceded us to New Orleans.

We had aboard all the sick who had been attacked by the scurvy, and the children, and the women, who nursed the unfortunates, undeterred by fear of the disease. If a stricken one was heard to complain, they came near, and their very presence soothed his pain. How affecting kindness is in the guise of beauty!

We did not lose one of our comrades, for the aid which they received in New Orleans, rest and abundant food, soon restored them to health. We forgot some of the hardships we had endured, and our recital of them seemed dreamlike. It was hard to believe that so many calamities could afflict men; and we were regarded with compassion when we passed along the street. How many tears our story caused to flow, we who looked as if we had returned from another world! The women above all, aroused pity, their pale features, melancholy aspect and weakened voices evoking a respect which cannot be described. People followed us with their eyes, as far as they could see us, and our every word was received with extraordinary eagerness. Kind Creoles! The refugees from Texas will never forget that you were more than friends, more than brothers to them!

Chapter Eight
DEPARTURE FROM NEW ORLEANS FOR FRANCE
CROSSING & ARRIVAL AT HAVRE

I STAYED ON SEVERAL DAYS AT
New Orleans, but finally home-sickness got the better of
me and I decided to return to France. The brig, *Edward of
Bordeaux*, captain, Alige, was to sail for Havre, and after
having made arrangements with him for my passage, I set
sail the 8th of March. Until the 19th, they were busy making repairs in the rigging, and we drifted with the current
as far as La Balise, at the mouth of the Mississippi. On the
20th we took aboard a pilot to steer us into the open sea,
but the wind and current drove us against the shore, where
we were obliged to anchor.

The pilot ordered the second anchor to be carried into
the open water to assist in floating us, but the wind would
not allow of this. He himself, with the boat, was thrown
across the cable and, together with four of our best soldiers
went under; but fortunately, we succeeded in saving them,
and then drew in the boat.

Nothing new happened to us until the 1st of April. On
the 2d we recognized the Los Rokos Bank, and came in
sight of the Cayo de Sal on the east quarter S.E. Longitude
83° 4, 5. Latitude 24.s.

On the 10th of April, we doubled the Bermuda Islands,
and until the 2d of May there was nothing new, with the

weather stormy and the seas high, for sounding showed sand with black spots at 83 fathoms.

On the 3rd of May, at 6 o'clock in the morning, we sighted the Scilly Islands; and at 8 the lantern of the ship showed us St. Agnes; towards noon the point of Lands' End showed itself to the northeast.

At 3 o'clock we sighted the light tower on the N. 8 miles in the distance.

We still sailed along the coast; at 6 o'clock we caught sight of the fires on Lizard Cape and Point New Keyan and 10 o'clock saw the lights of the Plymouth beacon. Rounded Star Point and Point Hope at a distance of 9 miles.

On the 7th of May, rounded Portland Point on the N.N.E.

In the evening, being near the Alderney Islands on the S.S.E., we put about.

On the 8th, at 7 o'clock in the morning, we rounded the Cape de Hague on the S.S.E.

On the 9th of May, at 3 o'clock in the afternoon, we took the pilot aboard and spread sails for Le Havre.

At 8 o'clock we turned to the S.E. a quarter E. in order to pick up the lights of Le Heve. The weather was superb.

On the 10th we anchored in the roadstead of Le Havre and a health official was sent aboard to keep us in quarantine.

When this was over, we went ashore; and when I touched again the soil of my native country my joy was difficult of expression. After many vicissitudes, I was to be restored to my family and enjoy the repose and tranquillity I had vainly sought in the new world, and, cured of the mania for traveling, I could say with Virgil:

> "*Per varios casus, per tot discrimina rerum*
> *Forsan et haec olim meminisse juvabit.*"

Chapter Nine
MILLARD'S JOURNAL
DEPARTURE FROM PARIS
ARRIVAL AT BORDEAUX
EMBARKATION & CROSSING
ARRIVAL AT PHILADELPHIA

I WAS IN PARIS WITHOUT EM-
ployment, having resigned from the Army, enjoying a very
modest income; my time slipped by with a monotonous
and boring uniformity. After having spent a portion of my
life in the midst of the tumult of the camps, and finding myself incapable of devoting myself to other occupations, and
being unable longer to support this idle state, I decided to
leave Europe, to go to America, and there to join the French
Refugees who were founding a colony in Texas. This last
decision was not the result of discontent; for it was with
pleasure that I saw the French Government strengthen itself in the confidence and the love of the French people.
I was urged on by that curiosity which at times governs a
man who is free and master of his own destinies. Although
I was not entirely without personal ties, having put my
affairs in order, I left Paris a-foot on the 18th of November,
1817, headed for Bordeaux and arrived in that city on the
29th of the same month.

I shall not speak of my stay in Bordeaux. The ship, *The Hunter*, of Philadelphia, was about to set sail, and after making arrangements to cross on the boat, I boarded her, together with several Frenchmen. Madame Vasquez, wife of the Spanish colonel of this name, was aboard and bore with much courage and strength the fatigues and dangers to which we were exposed during the crossing. We had several blows which as many times almost shipwrecked us. These preliminaries did not bespeak good luck, but as I am not superstitious, and had for a long time been accustomed to facing death on the field of battle, death could not dismay me on the bosom of the deep, and the tempest appeared to me less to be feared than gunpowder, shell, and grapeshot.

Finally, after having long been the plaything of the wind and waves, our vessel entered the harbor of Philadelphia, on the 4th of May, 1818.

We disembarked, and, as soon as I was ashore, I sought Mr. Dirat, Secretary of the French Society, for whom I had letters of recommendation; these I presented to him and was welcomed with especial kindness. He, knowing the reason for my voyage, told me the French refugees had been gone for several days, having at their head Generals Lallemand, brothers; that they were going to the Province of Texas to establish there a colony which was to have the name of Champ d'Asile. He also apprised me of the fact that I would be obliged to remain in Philadelphia until a new contingent of French should leave for Texas, at the same time offering me his services and promising to do everything to make my life agreeable. I can not say too much of his kindness and the proofs of friendship which he gave to all with whom he came in contact.

I had time to visit Philadelphia, its public buildings and, above all, its port, where there is constant activity and where the flags of all nations are to be seen. I admired the industry of this people whose freedom the French insured, who employ this liberty only to further its prosperity by each day widening its commerce. The Americans, thanks to the good sense which guides them, will soon become one of the most formidable maritime powers of the world, and will rival, without pursuing the same methods, the people whose yoke they threw off. As I strolled along the docks, I recalled Telemachus, discoursing with Narbal on the commerce and government of the Phoenicians.

Fortunate country, said I to myself, you have gone through a revolution, but it is all over. Those who sought to impose their laws on you were obliged to restore to you those rights, yours from God, which they tried to wrest from you, and which you enjoy in the midst of peace. You now afford an asylum to the sons of those who shed their blood for your independence, and it was such thoughts as these that led me to bless the memory of Washington and Franklin, and to give heed to the memory of those Frenchmen who were their friends and their rivals in glory.

General Henry Lallemand soon returned to Philadelphia in order to take to Champ d'Asile the French who had stayed behind, together with those who were arriving almost daily in that city. I was associated with several of these, and amongst us there existed the greatest intimacy, each of us having but one desire; to work for the prosperity of the colony, and collectively but one wish: that success should crown our efforts.

I went to see General Lallemand and was welcomed with

that frank kindness which characterized him. I begged him in the name of my friends—who had so charged me—to inform me as to what was necessary to be done.

The General told me to advise them to be ready to leave for Texas at any moment, and to make their plans accordingly. After a rather long talk with the General, in which I had the opportunity to observe that he joined to the widest information a mellowed philosophy and rare modesty, I left him, and went immediately to report the result of my mission to my friends, telling them we would soon be leaving for our new country.

Each then abandoned himself to his thoughts, and spoke of his plans and the scheme of life he had formulated, based on his conception of the place we were to inhabit; and there was not one among us who did not see in the future inexhaustible happiness and content.

Chapter Ten

DEPARTURE FROM PHILADELPHIA
ARRIVAL AT NEW ORLEANS
DEPARTURE FOR TEXAS
ARRIVAL IN THE COLONY

THE GENERAL, WHO LOST sight of nothing and showed as much energy in the execution of his projects as sagacity in their conception, hired a ship to transport us to New Orleans and we left the 10th of May, arriving the first of June, 1818. Madame Vasquez, who accompanied us, fell ill during the voyage, and in spite of the desire she felt to rejoin her husband, it was impossible for her to think of leaving New Orleans, her illness growing more grave, until we despaired of her life. This lady gave us every moment an example of the greatest courage, and can be cited as a model of conjugal love.

On the 4th of June, thanks to the attention and solicitude of M. Lafitte, a resident of New Orleans, who secured us everything needed for our voyage, we went down the Mississippi which flows into the Gulf of Mexico near La Balise, and we headed straight for Galveston.

We were approaching the end of our voyage, and on the 14th of June, 1818, we arrived at Champ d'Asile, where we were reunited to our comrades in glory and misfortune.

173

How can one depict, express, or convey an idea of the way in which we were received by General-in-Chief Lallemand, General Rigaud, and all the members of the colony. A father does not view with more joy and delight his dear children, brothers do not meet again with more pleasure. The General pressed us all to his breast with an expression of the warmest friendship; and wishing to calm our fears as to our fate and to make certain himself that we would be as comfortable as circumstances and surroundings would permit, he assigned us to the several cohorts.

The colony was organized on a military basis, the strictest discipline existing, having as its basis friendship and confidence.

The fortifications which were to insure the safety of the colony and to protect us from attacks by neighboring peoples had already begun. As early as the day after our arrival, we set to work, and all the refugees, without distinction of rank or grade, were busy there. The General-in-Chief and other superiors themselves afforded an example, and each vied with the other in zeal, activity and devotion. We rested only when rest was indispensable, for we were persuaded that by putting ourselves in a position of practical defense we were taking a step in the direction of the happiness which could be assured only by the peace of the colony. I used moments of rest to make observations of the country that I was destined to inhabit, and I shall set these down, imperfect as they may be.

Chapter Eleven

GEOGRAPHICAL LOCATION OF TEXAS, AND ITS EXTENT
ITS SOIL, ITS CLIMATE, ITS LAKES, ITS RIVERS
ITS POPULATION

THE PROVINCE OF TEXAS, SITuated in the most northerly and easterly portion of the dependency of San Luis Potosi, in Mexico, touches on the north the wild country of Louisiana; on the east, New Orleans; on the south, the Gulf of Mexico; on the west, Santander and Coahuila, separated by the Del Norte River. Texas extends between 27° and 38° latitude, and between 96° and 100° longitude, meridian of Paris. But since it is irregular, it varies from north to south from 75 to 150 leagues; its length from east to west is from 135 to 140 leagues. Texas was discovered in 1522 by the Spanish, who made successive voyages there in 1528 and 1539, and the French founded a colony there in 1535, under the reign of Francis I, but were expelled by the Spanish in 1595.

The coastline of Texas is low, sandy and swampy. As one goes into the interior, he finds vegetation and a great quantity of shrubs; but to find fertile land one has to go from thirty to forty leagues. The temperature of Texas is that of the south of France, and many trees preserve their foliage throughout the year.

Texas is crossed by a great number of rivers; the Sabine which bounds it on the east, and the Barosso on the N.E. which flows into the Gulf of Mexico near Galveston Bay. The surrounding country offers enchanting views, carpets of green adding to the richness of the landscape, while beautiful plants and the rarest birds made this section a delightful spot.

Forests, which the ax has spared until the present day, cover a part of Texas, and from time to time prairies are found, where European crops could be grown. Through the foliage of trees a column of smoke often betrays the presence of savages. A great number of animals and wild beasts are encountered in these forests, above all the wild horses, which the natives have been skillful enough to capture and tame.

There are still to be found in Texas many rattlesnakes; the congo and the egg-eater are likewise very numerous, several of the colonists having been bitten by the reptiles. Only one was in anywise disabled, he having been treated for the bite before we discovered its proper remedy. This remedy is a root which grows abundantly on the plains, and its identification by the Indians is not the least of the services they rendered us.

The population of Texas, before we established ourselves there, numbered about 7000 souls. The wild tribes of the *Tankards*, the *Panis*, *Apaches*, and *Camanches* often showed themselves near the frontiers of the country, and, if they were not withheld by threats and fear, they gave themselves up to outrages.

The *Karankavès* were a barbarous tribe of cannibals, constantly on the move. It was they who, having surprised two of our unfortunate comrades, devoured them—the remains of their quivering limbs were found still on the ground. The most important posts are those situated on the Trinity, and Naquidoches, situated on a little stream which empties into the Toya in the center of Texas.

The choice that General Lallemand had made of Texas as a suitable place for the founding of a colony led one to hope that success would crown his efforts. With the Gulf of Mexico on one side, the Sabine and Baosso Rivers on the other, and between them two other streams and prairies, ample supplies were insured by means of frequent communications with the continent as well as with other nations. Through what fatality did we fail? We lacked neither courage nor strength. Fate should not have persecuted us. If it accords its favors to those who live a blameless life, who could have a greater claim on its bounty than Frenchmen who have always been faithful to flag and honor, who expatriated themselves only to live in peace from the fruits of their labors, and whose sole wealth consisted of memories? Had they disturbed their country? No; they wished to oppose themselves to its slavishness and repulse for the last time those whom for twenty-five years they had repeatedly defeated. Destiny betrayed them, and they succumbed; if only France might be happy, they would bless their defeat, and echoes of Texas would learn to repeat the sacred words: Honor and Country, which are engraved on the bark of trees whose tops tower toward heaven; and those who shall visit those countries which we have been compelled to abandon will give homage, we are certain, to the generous sentiments which animate the French.

I will not go into any great detail as to the advantages of Texas. Nor shall I repeat what M. Hartmann has had to say in his journal of all our misfortunes. Having escaped as if by a miracle from all those scourges which assailed us, what thanks do we not owe to Providence! I left Galveston Island and embarked for New Orleans on a boat commanded by Captain Devis, whom chance led into those parts and who saved me from a death which would have soon stricken me, since I was without resources. What obligations am I not under to him! With what kind generosity did he receive me!

We anchored in New Orleans in the month of October, 1818. The inhabitants of that city were generous with all possible attentions, giving me both clothes and money; and it is to them that I owe the happiness of seeing my country again.

I left New Orleans to return to France, after having expressed my thanks to the colonists who had so generously aided me. It is a pleasant duty to set down here their names. They are: Messrs. Dubueys, Fortier, Michel—thus can I partially repay the debt I owe them. After a fortunate crossing, I landed at Nantes the 3rd of May 1819, and I am now sharing the happiness that the French owe to a monarch whose new benefits they are daily learning to appreciate.

Epilogue

WHEN WE LEFT WE LEARNED that General Lallemand had retired to a dwelling about ten leagues from New Orleans, which he had purchased. General Rigaud was on his death bed, his daughter was a teacher in a private home at Opelousas and his son a clerk in a business house.

Most of the Texas colonists, without work and consequently a prey to the greatest poverty, languished in New Orleans, desiring to return to a country which several among them had but too lightly quitted. All were most anxious to devote to her their days which they now found all the more precious since they had had the misfortune to spend part of them away from her.

It is only fair for the subscribers to the Champ d'Asile Fund to remember that is was no other than these very refugees that they tried to help. Since their purpose was not achieved, how much better it now is to restore these colonists to happiness by bringing them again to their homes than to have aided them on a distant shore, where the silence of despair would stifle the gratitude whose happy expression their benefactors may now easily hear.

We cannot bring this epilogue to a close without begging our readers' pardon for not having given them the story which we had promised, of the love of Edward and Adrienne. Being unfamiliar with literature, we consulted a man of letters, who advised us that such an account of a romantic affair would belie our preface. The chief object of our work is to make known the causes of our failure; to set them forth in strictest truths so that eventually, feeling people may hasten to the relief of our unfortunate companions, and restore to the fatherland Frenchmen who have never ceased to be such, for death alone—as chance a thing as birth—can take away distinction which no living man would willingly renounce.

Finis

THREE HUNDRED COPIES OF THIS
BOOK HAVE BEEN PRINTED FOR
MEMBERS OF THE BOOK CLUB OF
TEXAS BY THE RYDAL PRESS, SANTA
FE, NEW MEXICO. THE TYPE
USED IS MONOTYPE
PERPETUA

1937

The above colophon was printed in the original. It is reproduced here in facsimile as a part of the original book and indicates why copies of the original are so rare.

The above device was designed for the Book Club by Mr. David R. Williams, Vice President of the Club. Appropriately, it is composed of the cattle brands of some of the early Texas ranches and, in a way, these brands represent the first form of printing done in Texas.

The central figure in the device is the branding iron of the colonizer, Stephen Fuller Austin, who brought the first Anglo Saxon culture to Texas and who set up at San Felipe de Austin a printing press. The brands at the top and bottom of the device are . . . the Maverick brand, the Half Circle Ten, the Spanish brand of José Antonio Navarro, the O K brand, the initials of the Book Club of Texas designed in the spirit of the early cattle brands, and the brand of the O B Ranch.

Facsimile from the Original Announcement of The Book Club of Texas

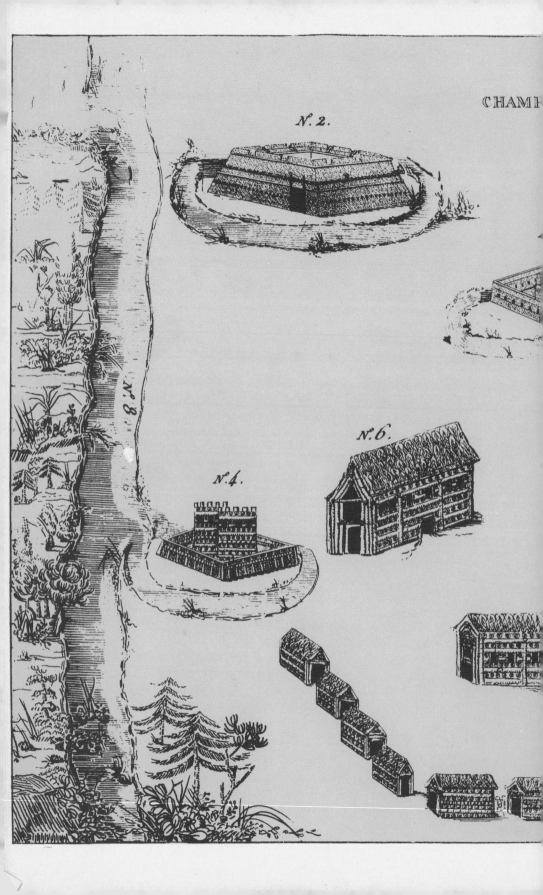

N. 2.

N.°8.

N. 4.

N.°6.